# LOVE walks by FAITH

Also by Charlie Osburn
*The Charlie Osburn Story*
Copyright © 1986
by Charlie Osburn and Fred Lilly

# LOVE walks by FAITH

*We Gave It All to Jesus*

Charlie and Jeanne Osburn

Edited by Cheryl Denton
Harvey Whitney Books
Cincinnati, Ohio

Published by
Harvey Whitney Books Company
4906 Cooper Road
Cincinnati, Ohio, 45242 USA

Copyright © 2007 by Harvey Whitney Books Co.
All rights reserved.

Cover design: The cover of this book is symbolic of Charlie and Jeanne Osburn's Christian walk. Their names appear at the foot of the cross of Jesus to whom they gave their lives.
   They learned that becoming fully alive in Christ means walking daily to the foot of the cross and giving everything to Jesus. They put all of their faith in God to give them back the only things they really need: the power of the Holy Spirit, salvation through Christ Jesus, and God's great mercy and love.

All Scripture references contained in this book are taken from the HOLY BIBLE, NEW INTERNATIONAL VERSION®. Copyright © 1973, 1978, 1984 by International Bible Society. Used by permission of Zondervan. All rights reserved.

The stories in this book are all true. In order to protect the privacy rights of the individuals involved in the stories, most names in this book and some details surrounding the stories have been changed. Any real names in the stories have been used with permission. These real names can be recognized by the use of both first and last names when a person's story is discussed.

Compiled and edited by Cheryl Denton

Library of Congress Control Number: 2006932601

ISBN 0-929375-29-7 (paperback)

Printed and bound in the United States of America
www.harveywhitneybooks.com

## CONTENTS

Foreword  *7*
1 Separated From God by Sin  *9*
2 Jesus Was Calling  *17*
3 You've Got to Give It All to Jesus!  *27*
4 Charlie, Do You Trust Me?  *39*
5 Lord, What Are You Doing to Us?  *49*
6 My Mission in Life  *59*
7 Walking in Faith  *63*
8 On the Road for Jesus  *73*
9 Learning to Love as Jesus Does  *87*
10 The Remedy for Fear  *101*
11 A Change in Plans  *109*
12 A New Mission From God  *115*
13 Help for the Hurting  *121*
14 Lessons From Christ  *131*
15 We Are All Evangelists  *141*
A Personal Message to the Reader  *149*
Epilogue  *151*

# FOREWORD

I have often heard it said that the easiest way to make God laugh is to tell him that you have plans. In 1982, I had great plans for the business my partner and I were developing. Then I attended one of Charlie's week-long parish missions. He talked about giving up a flourishing business and devoting his life to preaching the Good News.

Obviously he touched a part of my soul. Within a few months I had done virtually the same thing and entered a seminary. A seed which had been planted by my pastor was watered by Charlie's words!

Fast forward to 2005. I hadn't had any contact with Charlie since that week in 1982. By now I was pastor of St. Anne's Parish in Pensacola, Florida. Someone just happened to mention that Charlie was now retired and living in Pensacola. He had made plans to spend his remaining years relaxing in the Florida sun and fishing.

Again, God laughed at someone having made plans. I looked Charlie up, and we had a grand reunion. Since that time he has revived the School of Evangelization and has been working out of our parish on the west side of Pensacola. As we work together to spread the good news of God's love, we often laugh in amazement at how a chance meeting 25 years ago changed the plans of two men who now enjoy the opportunity to share the ministry that was in God's plan all along!

Father Jack

Very Reverend John F. Gray, VF
5200 Saufley Field Road
Pensacola, FL 32526

CHAPTER ONE

# Separated From God by Sin

## Charlie Remembers His Early Years

I would like to tell you how Jesus Christ came into my life. Before God could bless me in this way, though, I had to learn some very important lessons about life. I learned them the hard way.

We all come into the world the same way, created by God and born of human parents. God creates us for a purpose—to know him, to love him, and to serve him. But none of this was communicated to me as a boy, born in 1933 in a small town in North Carolina.

> ■ α ■
> **God creates us for a purpose.**
> ■ Ω ■

My mother and father were very loving, but not particularly religious. I suppose my parents believed in God—I remember his name coming up in conversation once in a while. But, except for occasional weddings and funerals, we never went to church.

At a very early age, the things of the world began to excite me. Material possessions brought me what I thought was happiness. Money in the pocket, spending money, selling things for profit—these were the things that brought me joy and fulfillment. Making money became my definition of the purpose of life. Money itself became my god. So, I decided that I would find ways to make as much money as possible.

I quickly learned that I had a knack for making money. One of my earliest successes was selling lemonade during World War II when I was eight years old. Sugar was rationed then, but my family received a greater ration of sugar than most, because my father was in the service. I made lemonade with real sugar in a big wooden washtub and pulled it on a wagon down to the tobacco market. People loved that ice-cold lemonade, sweetened with sugar, on hot days. I made a big profit, and it excited me a great deal. My pockets were loaded, so I was happy.

My mom was a great mother, always encouraging the six of us kids. She would say, "If you want something done, give it to Charlie. He can do anything."

I felt like King Kong. I really believed that I could do anything.

As I grew older and more successful, I began to think about God. I decided that God liked successful people. My spiritual philosophy was 'God helps those who help themselves.' I found it quite easy to help myself. Not only was it easy for me to make money, but people admired me for it. Some were even jealous. Thrusting my chest out like a proud peacock, I'd show off my new car and bulging wallet. When I noticed that people were admiring or envious, I showed off even more openly. I wanted people to notice Charlie Osburn.

My father was in the Army, and when I was sixteen years old, he left for the Korean War. When I watched him walk away, my heart just about broke. I made up my mind that I would join him there when I turned seventeen. While he was away, I was the man of the family.

I joined the Navy at seventeen, and I never did get sent to Korea. But I trained a lot of guys who did. Most of them never came back. Thank God my dad did. I spent ten years in the military, pulling extra duty and cutting hair to fatten my paycheck.

When I was transferred to Pensacola, Florida, in 1955, I arrived at the Naval Station to present my transfer orders. A very pretty young woman named Jeanne finished processing my papers, and I asked her to direct me to a restaurant where I could get a good hamburger. When I arrived at the restaurant, Jeanne was there with some of her friends. They asked me to sit with them, and I was attracted to Jeanne from that moment on.

> ■ α ■
> **Religion had never meant anything to me.**
> ■ Ω ■

Jeanne and I dated and finally decided to get married. Because I loved Jeanne so much, I wanted to understand and appreciate every aspect of her life, but I just couldn't understand why she was so committed to the Catholic Church. Religion had never meant anything to me. As we discussed our future life together, she told me that she would continue to be active in her church. She also insisted that we raise our children in the Catholic faith.

Because of Jeanne's commitment to her faith, I decided to investigate the Catholic Church. I began talking with the principal of Pensacola Catholic High. The principal taught me a great deal about the church and displayed the same intense devotion to it as my wife-to-be. So, for the first time in my life, I began to think seriously about committing my life to God and to a church.

Later, I was transferred to a Naval base in Sanford, Florida, and was separated from Jeanne for a while. This gave me more time to think about our future. I decided to take instructions at the local Catholic parish and at the end of the course—only a few weeks before our wedding—the priest baptized me in a private ceremony.

I didn't know why I was so drawn to the church. It wasn't a personal love for Jesus that I had. It was a great love for the awesomeness and the vastness and the great unity of the church. At the age of twenty-three, I had been all over the world. I thought the Catholic Church was an amazing organization.

"I've got a surprise for you," I told Jeanne when I returned to Pensacola a few days before our wedding. "I am now a baptized Catholic."

Jeanne was thrilled. She picked up the phone and called the priest who was supposed to perform the wedding ceremony and arranged for a nuptial Mass. In 1956, the church did not permit Masses during a marriage ceremony unless both partners were Catholic. Our wedding day was truly glorious.

> **I told Jeanne, "I am now a baptized Catholic."**

Over the next twelve years, I felt as if I had the world by the tail. Jeanne gave me five children in the first six years of our marriage—three boys and two girls. During that time, we took on the task of running one of the restaurants that Jeanne's mother and her uncles had worked very hard to develop into a Pensacola landmark—Mama Nunnari's.

I became very active in the community and in the church. Eventually, I was appointed honorary mayor of Warrington, a suburb of Pensacola, Florida, where we lived. Business at the restaurant just got better with each passing year, and before long, I made my first million. I didn't think anything could stop me. I wasn't on my way to the top. I had arrived.

Then a tragedy happened in my life. In 1968, when I was thirty-five years old, I discovered that my neighbor had raped my six-year-old daughter. This same man had been molesting both my daughter and my eight-year-old son for two years. I became angry with God. I was so angry and filled with so much hate, that I was angry with everyone. I was angry with the priest and angry with the church. I began to pull away from the church and not participate in the functions.

> **I discovered that my neighbor had raped my six-year-old daughter.**

At thirty-five years old, I began to drink. I began to do other things that I had never done before. I went crazy at home. I accused Jeanne and the other children of not watching over the two little ones. I tried to escape the diabolical evil of what had happened by condemning everyone in sight.

Jesus said in Luke 6:38, "Give, and it will be given to you. A good measure, pressed down, shaken together and running over, will be poured into your lap. For with the measure you use, it will be measured to you." We often think of this verse in a positive light, imagining a bountiful sack of grain overflowing with goodness. But imagine what would happen if that sack were filled with hate, pressed down, shaken together and running over. I had hate pouring into my lap, because I had measured out so much of it to my neighbor, my wife, and my kids.

> **I was really angry at God. And I was full of hate.**

I hated my neighbor with such a passion, that I wanted to kill him. I took him through the court system, but they only gave him three years probation. That made me angry at the court system. I became angry with all authority. I even became angry with myself.

Church became a hollow empty nothing. I went to church only because it was convenient in my life as a politician. It was good for business, because I owned a very large restaurant close by. And it was always good to go to church and let everybody see me. My life with the Lord was totally and completely empty. I was alienated against the church, and I hated everybody.

There are a lot of unbelievers. We even have a lot of them in the church. I was one of them. I was really angry at God. And I was full of hate. Hatred will kill you. There is no greater poison than bitterness. It's just a matter of time before it will kill you.

After eight years of hatred, I developed a lot of sickness. The pressure in my life was intense. After my children were molested, I began to drink 'just a little to settle my nerves.' The demands of business, politics, social life, and family responsibilities added up to eighteen-hour days, seven days a week. I thought I needed a little nip now and then. I told myself I deserved it.

But the more responsibilities I took on, the more my family life grew strained, and the more heavily I began to drink to relieve the pressure. I became an alcoholic, but I denied it. I blamed my problems on everyone else—my wife, my children, my neighbor, the IRS—but never on myself. I drank and partied so much that I became known as the 'wild man of Warrington.'

One morning in 1976, I remember waking up and feeling disillusioned with the whole world. There I was a millionaire, successful in the eyes of everyone who knew me. But I was an empty, broken man, and I knew it. Nothing could satisfy me. The harder I worked and the more money I made, the more money I wanted. It was the same with my drinking. The more I drank, the more it took to satisfy me. It was even true of my smoking—first a pack a day, then two packs, then three packs.

> ■ α ■
> **I was an empty, broken man, and I knew it. Nothing could satisfy me.**
> ■ Ω ■

Caught in this vicious cycle, I found myself at forty-three with high blood pressure, a hiatal hernia, and a number of nervous conditions. I ate Valium all day long to keep my hands from shaking so I could play golf.

I had lived a charmed life for nearly twenty years, but now I felt awful. I began to realize that my choices in life had led me to this. When I discovered what I had become, I was desperate. I knew something had to change, but even at that point, I never dreamed that the very money and success I had always craved were causing many of my problems. My hatred towards my neighbor only added fuel to the fire.

> ■ α ■
> **I found the perfect scapegoat in my wife.**
> ■ Ω ■

I looked for someone to blame, and I found the perfect scapegoat in my wife, Jeanne. *She's the problem,* I thought. *In twenty years, she hasn't done a thing for me except spend my money and give me a hard time.*

Our relationship deteriorated to the point where we had absolutely nothing to talk about. I'd leave the house in the morning and come home at night without ever saying a word to her. If I was leaving town for two or three days, I wouldn't tell her. I would just come home, change my clothes, reload my pockets with money, and leave without so much as a nod in her direction.

So, I began to plan how to leave her. I knew I had to proceed slowly. I was the mayor, after all. I couldn't let a scandal harm my chances for continued success and prestige.

## Jeanne Reflects Upon Their Early Life

When I stood next to Charlie on November 14, 1956, at St. Michael's Church in Pensacola, I said that I would take him "for better or worse, till death do us part." I pledged that I would spend the rest of my life with him. Those were words of faith. I didn't know what was in store for us. No couple does when they marry. I didn't know it at the time, but what I was really saying was that I was going to love Charlie, no matter what it cost me.

Many things had drawn me to Charlie since I had met him. One of the main reasons why I was confident about marrying him was that Charlie insisted that he would never drink alcohol. As a girl of nineteen, I was very impressed with that conviction. I didn't know very many men of twenty-three who were not drinking.

And do you know what happened? The man who said he would never drink began to drink. He drank so much that he became an alcoholic. As a result, my children and I were knocked around, used, and abused. That is the tragedy in many alcoholic homes.

> *My children and I were knocked around, used, and abused.*

During the worst days of his alcoholism, Charlie ran around with the 'jet set' of our town. Sometimes, while Charlie was out playing golf and having a good time, some of these 'friends' would visit and encourage me to divorce him.

"Charlie is never going to change," one would say. "You've got to teach him a lesson. Here's the name of a good lawyer. He'll take care of you."

It seemed strange that the same people my husband was wining and dining were the ones who were telling me to 'teach him a lesson' by divorcing him. I came very close to heeding their advice. I even went to see a lawyer and told him I wanted a divorce. When he had completed all the paperwork, I went to his office to sign it. But as I was riding up the elevator to the ninth floor to the lawyer's office, an inner voice said to me, "You're about to make a very big mistake."

By the time I walked into the lawyer's office, I knew in my heart that I would never put my signature on the divorce papers. I looked at the papers, then at the lawyer, and said, "I am really sorry that you've gone to all this effort, but this is the last place that I need to be this morning. I'm willing to pay you whatever you want for your efforts, but I'm not getting a divorce."

I wouldn't have said it this way at the time, but I made a decision to love Charlie just the way he was.

My mother met me at the door of our restaurant when I got back from the lawyer's office. As I greeted her, she asked what I had done. I smiled and said, "I'll tell you what I didn't do. I decided not to get a divorce."

> **I made a decision to love Charlie just the way he was.**

Mama smiled at me and said, "Let me tell you something, Jeanne. You're a lot stronger than I am."

That's all she said. My mother never tried to tell me what to do. She respected me as an adult, and she loved me. Her loving support gave me a great deal of the strength that she admired so much.

One day when I got home from working at our restaurant, I found a note on a very small piece of paper. The note was written by our son, Craig, who was seventeen years old at the time. It read, "Mom, why can't we be a loving family?"

As I read that note, I thought my heart was going to break. I realized how helpless I was. I had done everything I knew to improve our marriage and family. I had refrained from putting any kind of pressure on Charlie about how he spent his time or money. I had been very careful not to throw his misbehavior back at him by using angry words. I did whatever he wanted me to do, and I was always there for him when he wanted me.

> **"Oh, God, you've got to help me!"**

But none of it worked. I knew that night that I was totally helpless. When I went to bed with tears streaming down my face, I cried out, "Oh, God, you've got to help me!"

**Love**

¹If I speak in the tongues of men and of angels, but have not love, I am only a resounding gong or a clanging cymbal. ²If I have the gift of prophecy and can fathom all mysteries and all knowledge, and if I have a faith that can move mountains, but have not love, I am nothing. ³If I give all I possess to the poor and surrender my body to the flames, but have not love, I gain nothing.

⁴Love is patient, love is kind. It does not envy, it does not boast, it is not proud. ⁵It is not rude, it is not self-seeking, it is not easily angered, it keeps no record of wrongs. ⁶Love does not delight in evil but rejoices with the truth. ⁷It always protects, always trusts, always hopes, always perseveres.

⁸Love never fails. But where there are prophecies, they will cease; where there are tongues, they will be stilled; where there is knowledge, it will pass away. ⁹For we know in part and we prophesy in part, ¹⁰but when perfection comes, the imperfect disappears. ¹¹When I was a child, I talked like a child, I thought like a child, I reasoned like a child. When I became a man, I put childish ways behind me. ¹²Now we see but a poor reflection as in a mirror; then we shall see face to face. Now I know in part; then I shall know fully, even as I am fully known.

¹³And now these three remain: faith, hope and love. But the greatest of these is love.

**1 Corinthians 13:1–13**

CHAPTER TWO

# Jesus Was Calling

## Jeanne Meets Jesus

A few nights later, Charlie and I were working in our restaurant when a large party came in and asked to dine in our banquet room. Among this group were three young men who were dressed exactly alike. We were almost ready to close when they came in, and I was so busy getting things closed up for the night that I didn't pay much attention to the group. I knew that the waitresses were taking good care of them.

I did notice, however, that there was a lot of singing coming from that room. I couldn't resist walking over and listening. It was the three young men—brothers, I found out later—who were singing. They had wonderful voices. I mentioned to one of the waitresses that it would be nice if they would sing a song for us before they left.

A few minutes later she came to me and said, "They're ready to sing for us."

So I rounded up all the waitresses, cooks, busboys, and dishwashers, and we gathered around their table. They sang a popular love song for us. It was very nice.

When they finished, one of the young men looked at me and said, "We don't mind singing these kinds of songs, but we really like to sing about Jesus."

When he mentioned the name of Jesus, I felt a sweet sensation in my body. It was a very strange feeling. I had never heard anyone mention the name of Jesus in a public place like that before, and it really did something for me.

We all thanked the singers and then got back to work. I told the waitress not to charge the three brothers for their meals. A short time later, the party left, and we began finishing our chores so that we could go home.

Not even a full minute after the singers' party had walked out the front door, the three brothers came back in. They had learned that I had paid for their dinners, and they wanted to thank me. I was standing behind the cashier's counter, and they encircled me and began singing the love song, 'I Believe.' When they reached the line that says, "I believe that someday, someone will come and show me the way," they changed the words and instead sang, "I believe that Jesus will come and show me the way."

It happened again! When they sang the name of Jesus, I felt as though a light bulb had been turned on in my heart.

> **When they sang the name of Jesus, I felt as though a light bulb had been turned on in my heart.**

They told me that they were called the Stone Brothers and were gospel singers from out of town. They said they would be in Pensacola again, performing at a church a few months later.

Because of the busyness of our lives and the increasing tension between Charlie and me, I forgot all about the Stone Brothers. But one morning, as I was reading the newspaper, I came across an advertisement that announced the Stone Brothers were coming to town for a concert. I asked Charlie to go to the church with me to see them, but he initially refused. I countered with a request that we at least stop by on our way home from the restaurant so I could run in and say hello to them. When he found out that the concert would be over by the time we arrived, he gave in and agreed to go.

When we got to the church, Charlie decided he wanted to go in after all. When the Stone Brothers saw me, they sang another song for us. Charlie was flabbergasted by all the attention I was receiving. The Stone Brothers asked us to bring our entire family to the concert the next night, and to my surprise, Charlie agreed. But the next evening, when it was time to get ready to leave, Charlie was nowhere in sight. The children and I dressed and went to the church by ourselves. Seconds before the concert was supposed to begin, Charlie slipped into the seat beside me.

The Stone Brothers came out and began to sing a number called, 'A Song Was Born When I Met Jesus.' As I listened to them, I knew that something was indeed taking place in me. During the concert, they sang, played trumpets, and offered testimonies about what the Lord had done for them. Then, towards the end, they invited everyone present who wanted to 'make Jesus Lord of their lives' to come forward to pray.

It was my first experience with an altar call. I didn't respond, because I was afraid they would want me to join the Baptist Church. I knew, though, that I desperately needed to have Jesus in my life. I knew that I needed to surrender all my problems to him. Only he could help me.

As one of the Stone Brothers recited 'the sinner's prayer' for those who had gone forward, I followed along silently. Almost immediately, a sense of peace and security that I had never known before enveloped me. I was certain that Jesus had heard my plea and that he had entered my life in a new way.

> **I knew that I desperately needed to have Jesus in my life.**

After the concert, the brothers came to our house for supper. As they stood in the kitchen talking with me while I prepared the meal, I wanted to tell them what had happened to me during their concert. But I couldn't. I knew that Charlie wouldn't be able to handle any major change in my life, so I kept quiet about what I had experienced.

However, the Lord enabled me to love Charlie in a new way. I had never stopped loving my husband, no matter how cruel he had become. But God showed me how to love him in a spiritual way, as well as in an emotional way. I was able to relate to Charlie without pressuring him, and I was freed of the anger and resentment that had burned in my heart. The Lord enabled me to forgive Charlie completely for the things he had done.

> **The Lord enabled me to forgive Charlie completely.**

Our natural reaction when someone mistreats us is to resent both the action and the person. But the Lord wants us to let go of resentments and to forgive others. Unconditional forgiveness is the Christian way of life, and the Lord himself enables us to forgive in this way. I'm not a great saint. The change in my attitude was a miracle of grace. I had to struggle and, at times, bite my tongue. But the Lord and his grace were there for me.

This was especially true on a Sunday a few weeks after the Stone Brothers' concert. It was our twentieth wedding anniversary, and Charlie had left town. He had decided to become a real estate agent in order to earn more money. The exam, which was being given in another part of Florida, was not until Monday, but Charlie left on Sunday. I knew he had purposely planned to be away on our anniversary just to be spiteful. It hurt a great deal, and I had no one to turn to but Jesus.

While the children and I were at Mass that morning, my attention was continually drawn to the crucifix behind the altar. Each time I looked at it, it seemed to grow larger. When it did, I experienced the love of Jesus flowing into my heart. Finally, after thinking about Charlie, I prayed, "Lord, I've tried to change my husband for twenty years, and I've been unable to do it. I've given my own life to you, and I give Charlie to you, too."

> **It was a profound spiritual experience, which I later realized was the baptism of the Holy Spirit.**

Just then, the choir began singing a hymn called, 'Let There Be Peace on Earth.' The Lord's love and grace flooded into my heart. It was a profound emotional and spiritual experience, which I later realized was the baptism of the Holy Spirit. At the time, I only knew that the great Lord loved me enough to answer my prayer. I was on cloud nine.

When I went forward to receive Jesus in the bread that we as Catholics believe is the body of Christ, the Lord gave me a greater love for Charlie. I knew that this love could help create an opening for God to begin working in Charlie's life, too. I returned to my seat and began to cry. Jesus had worked a great healing in me, and I wanted to tell someone. How I wished I could go home and tell Charlie!

As soon as we got home, I phoned Charlie at his motel. When he answered, I said, "Honey, I want you to know that I love you just the way you are and that it doesn't matter to me where you go or how long you stay or who you go with. I'll be waiting for you." Then I hung up.

Charlie told me later that he just stood there in the motel room, not knowing what to do. When he first heard my voice on the phone, he had expected me to tell him that he was a sorry excuse for a man and that three lawyers would be waiting for him when he returned.

He would have known how to handle that. But he didn't know how to handle love or how to respond to it.

## Charlie Encounters Jesus

One day, my old friend, Father James Smith, walked into my restaurant. He and I had first met when I joined the Catholic Church in 1956. We had been friends for a number of years until he was assigned to a parish somewhere else.

I said, "How long has it been since you left Pensacola?"

"Fourteen years."

"I'm so glad to see you," I said.

"Well, praise the Lord, Charlie. It's exciting to see you, too."

I ignored the 'praise the Lord.' I asked, "How have you been?"

"Wonderful," he said.

That startled me. When I asked that question, most people would tell me how terrible their lives were, playing what I call the 'Ain't It Awful Game.'

'Oh, it's just awful, Charlie. Don't know if I'm going to make it. I've got problems at home, problems with my business, problems down at city hall. Ain't it awful?'

So that's what I did with Father Smith—for about two hours. I went on and on about what a terrible state my life was in.

After my monologue, he looked me in the eye and said, "Charlie, I've got good news for you."

*He wants to lend me some money.* I was convinced that priests carried a good amount of cash around with them. Since I had just finished telling Father Smith that I had lost a great deal of money gambling on golf games, I thought he would advance me a few thousand to tide me over during my dry spell.

But he didn't. He said, "Why don't you come over to my place tomorrow? I've got some exciting things to tell you about the church."

■ α ■

"I've got some exciting things to tell you about the church."

■ Ω ■

I thought I was a good Catholic in those days, by my own definition. I went to Mass every Sunday, regardless of what I had done during the week. For several years, I had even gone to Mass every day. My fervor had lapsed quite a bit during the previous few years as my life had fallen apart. I kept going to church on Sundays, though, because I thought it would be bad for business if people noticed I stopped attending. For a mayor concerned with social standing and future political ambitions, it was important to be seen in church, especially if you've got a restaurant only three blocks away.

When Father Smith told me that the church had more to offer me, I didn't know what he meant. *I've done everything there is to do: Knights of Columbus, president of the Holy Name Society, Legion of Mary, and the Society of St. Vincent de Paul. I even take up the collection every Sunday. Why in the world is he telling me there is something more in this church? I've tried everything it has.*

I don't know why I accepted Father Smith's invitation to hear more about what the church had to offer. But I heard myself saying, "Okay, I'll be there."

The next day, I was knocking on the rectory door. I'll never forget that meeting. I wasn't ten feet inside when Father Smith pointed his finger at me and said, "Charlie, you've got to give it all to Jesus."

*What? Jesus doesn't want any of my problems. I'm a mess.*

But I only said, "Yes, Father." Like any good Catholic, I knew that no matter what a priest said to me, I should always be diplomatic. I didn't tell him that I didn't have the slightest idea what he was talking about. I went over to the couch and sat down, and he began to tell me things that I thought were really strange.

> ■ α ■
>
> "Charlie, do you know that Jesus loves you?"
>
> ■ Ω ■

"Charlie," he said, "do you know that Jesus loves you?"

"There's no way he can love me. I've done too many terrible things," I said.

"Oh, yes he does," Father Smith said.

"Father Smith," I said, "You know me, and God knows me. But he knows me a lot differently than you know me. And there is no way he can love me. He knows the kind of person I am and the kinds of things I have done."

"Charlie," he said, "I don't care what you've done. I don't care how bad you think you are. Jesus loves you in spite of yourself. Jesus loves you totally, completely, and unconditionally."

I had never heard a priest talk like that before. I asked, "Are you sure?"

"I'm sure," he said. "If you had been the only person living on this earth, Jesus would have come and died just for you."

*Me? No good, lying, cheating me?*

We talked for four hours. I listened to things that I had never heard before. At the end, Father Smith said, "Why don't you come back next week?"

"You know, I think I will," I said.

I remember going back to my restaurant. I sat down at the bar, got a scotch and water, and then looked over at my bartender. I said, "You know Ben, God loves you." I knew that if God loved me, there wasn't anybody he couldn't love.

Ben said, "How do you know?"

I had to think a minute. *How did I know?* Father Smith had just insisted that God loves me. I said, "Ben, God loves you, because he loves me."

He looked at me and said, "Yeah, if God could love you, he could love anything."

On Monday afternoon, I was knocking on the rectory door again. As soon as I walked inside, Father Smith said, "Charlie, you've got to give it all to Jesus."

> **I was dying spiritually.**

*How can I give Jesus anything?* In my mind, Jesus was the big 'eye in the sky,' carefully noting everything I did right, but mostly everything I did wrong. I had so many more wrongs than rights that God was punishing me. He was beating me to death, and I didn't know how to get him off of me.

I just couldn't accept this love concept of Father Smith's. It was too much. I knew this priest was a nice guy, and I was grateful to him for wanting to tell me nice things, but I just couldn't believe that Jesus would love me.

I also knew, though, that I was dying spiritually. I was desperate and full of despair. Still, I could not believe the things that would save my life. I was a drowning man, refusing to grab a life preserver, because I was sure it wouldn't hold my weight.

Father Smith was way ahead of me. He sat me down and said, "Do you remember when Pope Pius XII died in 1958?"

Actually, I didn't. I said, "Every few years a pope dies, and we get a new pope. Then he dies, and we get another new one." None of it meant much to me.

"Well," he said, "let me tell you what happened to Pope Pius XII. After he died, the College of Cardinals came together to select a new pope. They deliberated and prayed for many days, but they just could not agree on who should be the new pope. Ballot after ballot came and went, and still, they had no agreement. Finally, they decided to elect an old cardinal from Venice who would be the caretaker of the Vatican for a few years. The cardinals figured they would try again to elect someone who would be pleasing to the world after the old cardinal's death. This man, Cardinal Roncalli, became Pope John XXIII."

He continued, "Pope John prayed a great deal and earnestly listened to the Holy Spirit. His prayer produced in him the conviction that the Catholic Church needed fresh air. So, much to the surprise and chagrin of many of the cardinals who elected him pope, he called a council of the world's bishops to be held in Rome. And that council, the pope said, was to renew the fervor of the day of Pentecost in the church in our day."

*What does any of this have to do with me?* I didn't say this out loud, of course, but I thought it the whole time Father Smith was talking with such excitement about the pope and the council and all the signs and wonders that followed it.

I had just begun to wonder if he had forgotten who he was talking to when he said, "Charlie, *you* are the church."

"What?" I said. "The church is that big building down on Fifth and Main with the stained-glass windows and the beautiful crosses."

■ α ■

## Me? A living, breathing church?

■ Ω ■

"No, you are the church," he insisted. "The church is the people who use that big building to worship God. The church is all the individual men and women who come together to hear God's voice and receive his blessings."

I had never heard that before. Me? A living, breathing church? Me, with all my faults and problems, a temple of the Holy Spirit and a brother to Jesus Christ?

Father Smith then began to talk about the outpouring of the Holy Spirit that Catholics had been experiencing ever since that council. Then he stopped and said, "Why don't you come back next week?"

I had planned on this being the last of our little chats. But this talk about Pentecost and the Holy Spirit and ordinary people like me being the church intrigued me. I wanted to find out more. He had only told me part of the story, and I was hooked. I had to come back the next week to find out what happened. "Okay," I said, "I'll be here."

A week later, I returned, and the scene at the door was repeated once again. Father Smith said, "Charlie, you've got to give it all to Jesus."

I still couldn't see how anyone could give anything to Jesus, but I only said, "Yes, Father."

After I sat down, he looked at me and said, "Charlie, Jesus wants to heal your body."

*Oh no, is he a faith healer? Everyone knows that faith healers are phonies. God doesn't just do things like that. That's what doctors are for.*

"Jesus wants to deliver you from alcohol," he said.

*Well, I'm not sure I want to be delivered.*

"Jesus wants to heal your relationship with your wife."

"Now wait," I said, "I know that God is great and good, but even he can't heal that. My marriage is beyond healing. It's finished, and I'm not sure I would even want it healed."

"Jesus wants to introduce you to his love," he said.

I was really puzzled. I couldn't understand. I didn't know what love was. I had never really loved anyone, and I didn't know how to love. I knew how to take advantage of people. I knew how to make money. I could wheel and deal just about anybody out of just about anything. But I couldn't love anyone, not even my wife.

> ■ α ■
> **"Jesus wants to introduce you to his love."**
> ■ Ω ■

*Dear God, this poor priest is going down the tubes.*

I don't know if Father Smith knew how I was reacting, but he went on telling me that God had created everyone out of his great love. He said, "Charlie, you can turn to God for forgiveness and healing. You can live a new kind of life."

I didn't believe this. I didn't believe that God had created everyone to receive his blessings equally. I believed that he had created me a bit better than most people. After all, I had more money and more energy than most. And he was punishing me more than other people, because I had done more bad things.

I had gone to church every Sunday for more than fifteen years. I had heard hundreds of hours of sermons. But still, I did not understand. All my life, I had been greedy, selfish, and arrogant. I had justified my behavior to myself. I had demanded success from myself without ever considering the needs and desires of anyone else. I gave no thought to my wife or my children. I was a hard man, and now this priest was telling me that God could melt that hardness and give me something I couldn't earn, buy, or get in any other way.

Father Smith said, "Charlie, God can give you love and enable you to love other people. In that love, you can find real happiness."

> ■ α ■
> **Something was happening inside of me.**
> ■ Ω ■

I sat there, thinking, but still, I resisted.

He said, "Why don't you come back next Monday?"

*I'm supposed to go golfing on Monday.* But something was happening inside of me. I was in turmoil, drinking more heavily than ever. "All right, I'll see you next week," I said.

---

**God's Love and Ours**

[7]Dear friends, let us love one another, for love comes from God. Everyone who loves has been born of God and knows God. [8]Whoever does not love does not know God, because God is love. [9]This is how God showed his love among us: He sent his one and only Son into the world that we might live through him. [10]This is love: not that we loved God, but that he loved us and sent his Son as an atoning sacrifice for our sins. [11]Dear friends, since God so loved us, we also ought to love one another. [12]No one has ever seen God; but if we love one another, God lives in us and his love is made complete in us.

[13]We know that we live in him and he in us, because he has given us of his Spirit. [14]And we have seen and testify that the Father has sent his Son to be the Savior of the world. [15]If anyone acknowledges that Jesus is the Son of God, God lives in him and he in God. [16]And so we know and rely on the love God has for us.

God is love. Whoever lives in love lives in God, and God in him. [17]In this way, love is made complete among us so that we will have confidence on the day of judgment, because in this world we are like him. [18]There is no fear in love. But perfect love drives out fear, because fear has to do with punishment. The one who fears is not made perfect in love.

1 John 4:7–18

CHAPTER THREE

# You've Got to Give It All to Jesus!

## Charlie Surrenders His Life to Jesus

The next week, I returned to Father Smith's and knocked on the door. When I walked in, he was standing in the kitchen with his back to me. He wheeled around and shouted, "Charlie, you've got to give it all to Jesus!"

"Well," I shouted back, "you tell me what to give him, and I'll give it to him!"

"You've got to give him your wife."

"Man, he can have her."

"You've got to give him your kids."

"They're his," I said.

"Charlie, Jesus wants to be the Lord of your life."

"You tell me how to let Jesus be the Lord of my life," I said, "and I'll do it."

Father Smith told me to kneel down on the floor, and I did. He put his hand on my head and said, "Father, you promised to send the Holy Spirit to anyone who would ask." He looked at me and said, "Charlie, do you desire the Holy Spirit of God?"

I looked up at him and said, "I do."

"Father," he continued, "Charlie desires to make Jesus Christ the Lord of his life." He paused and said, "Don't you, Charlie?"

"Yes," I said.

■ α ■

**"Charlie, you've got to give it all to Jesus!"**

■ Ω ■

And he said, "Father, by faith, we receive your gift, and we thank you." Then he asked me something that I wished he hadn't. "How do you feel, Charlie?"

"I don't feel anything," I said.

Father Smith had described the Holy Spirit to me as someone who comes like a bolt of lightning. I was expecting something extraordinary and wonderful. As far as I could tell, nothing had happened.

In my disappointment, I thought I heard a voice saying, "You dirty, rotten, no-good lying bum, you'll never get it."

Then I heard another voice say, "God will never refuse anyone who seeks after the Holy Spirit."

> **I knew nothing about spiritual warfare.**

At that time, I knew nothing about spiritual warfare and the influence that Satan tries to exert on believers. But I knew which voice I wanted to believe.

I got up off the floor. As I walked to the door to go home, Father Smith said, "Charlie, we've got a prayer meeting at the church on Wednesday nights. Would you like to come?"

"What kind of meeting?" I asked.

"A prayer meeting."

It sounded very un-Catholic to me. "Does the bishop know about this?" I asked.

"Yes," he said, "The bishop knows all about it. He asked me to start it."

*If the bishop approved it, it must be all right. Still, a prayer meeting in our church seems strange. Maybe I'd better not go . . .* "I'll think about it," I said.

When I got home, I called Jeanne and the kids to sit down. I said, "I don't understand what Father Smith is telling me about the Holy Spirit. I don't understand this experience with Jesus Christ that he keeps talking about. But if what he's telling me is true, I can't afford to miss it. Now, would any of you like to go to the prayer meeting with me to receive whatever it is we're supposed to receive?"

Jeanne smiled at me and said, "I'll go."

But each of our five children refused. I'm sure they thought I was just on another crazy fling, working early for the next election to get the church vote.

When Wednesday night came around, Jeanne and I went to the prayer meeting. I walked into the room and saw people with their hands raised in the air. *What in the world is this? I am really in the wrong place! This is the silliest thing I have ever seen—all these people with their hands in the air and praying out loud.*

This went on for two hours. I just kept looking at my watch. *When does this thing end? I've got to get out of here.*

Even though I wanted to leave as fast as I could, I was intrigued by one strange thing. Every once in a while, Father Smith would boom out a message in a language I didn't understand. I knew that he could speak Latin, but I was surprised to hear him speak it so well.

Then another man I knew who only had a high school education like I did started speaking in Latin, just like Father Smith. *Now how did he ever learn Latin?*

I was growing very concerned. *If the people of Warrington ever hear about me being with people like this, I'll never get re-elected as mayor.*

I had been very careful all my life about my public image. Now, I thought, everything I had worked so hard for was in serious jeopardy.

As the meeting was winding down, one of the leaders asked if anyone needed prayer. *This is my opportunity.* "Sure," I said, "you can all pray for me." Then I gave everyone a big smile, grabbed Jeanne's hand, and headed for the door.

But before I got halfway across the room, a man put two chairs in front of us and said, "Have a seat."

"What for?" I asked.

"We're going to pray for you."

"Right here in front of everybody? You must be kidding."

"No, we're not kidding. We're going to pray for you right now." He smiled and motioned for us to sit down.

I was trapped, so I sat down on one chair, and Jeanne sat down on the other. Then, a number of people gathered around and put their hands on me. One woman knelt down in front of us and put her hand on my knee.

*This is nuts.*

Then they all prayed loudly for about fifteen minutes in English and in what I thought was Latin. After they were done, the woman whose hand was still on my knee looked up and spoke to me. "Charlie, how do you feel?"

"Terrible," I said, "I wish I weren't here. Right now, I honestly think that there may not even be a God. I feel like an empty hole."

So they prayed again, louder than ever. I glanced over at Jeanne, who was grinning from ear to ear. When they finally finished, I grabbed Jeanne's hand and left as fast as I could work my way through the room.

> **I thought constantly about my experience at the prayer meeting.**

For the next two days, I thought constantly about my experience at the prayer meeting. I finally figured out that the people at the meeting hadn't been speaking Latin at all. They had been praying in tongues, and I wanted no part of it. I was angry and embarrassed to think I had just sat there while people I knew babbled away in a language they didn't understand.

Father Smith, however, was persistent. Later that week, I went to another meeting at another Catholic Church and found that these people did the same bizarre things. My distaste increased when I saw an elderly woman sitting in the back wholeheartedly praising Jesus. She was very poor. *How can she do that when she's in rags?* It seemed incredible to me that she could talk about how good God was. It seemed unbelievable that she could love Jesus more than all the earthly treasure I had worked so hard to accumulate.

Father Smith knew that I was disgusted, embarrassed, and afraid to meet this new wave of the Spirit in the church. But instead of leaving me alone, he kept up his offensive. He called me one day and said, "Charlie, the church tells us to be ecumenical."

"What's that?"

"We're supposed to have fellowship with our Protestant brothers and sisters. I want you to come to a Protestant meeting with me."

> **"The church tells us to be ecumenical."**

"It's a sin to go to a Protestant service," I said.

"No, it's not," he said. "The bishops have told us very clearly to be open to Protestants."

"Father Smith," I said, "are you sure you're in good standing with the bishop?"

"I am."

"Well," I said, "which Protestant church do you want to go to?"

"The meeting is not at a church," he said. "It's over at the Holiday Inn."

*A service at the Holiday Inn!* I was stunned. Father Smith wanted me to go to a Protestant service at the same Holiday Inn where I went drinking with my friends. I didn't want to go, but I was too ashamed to tell Father Smith why.

Father Smith didn't give me any time to think about it. "I'll pick you up in fifteen minutes," he said, and he hung up.

I went to the Holiday Inn with Father Smith. I looked down at the floor as we passed the bar. I felt as if all my buddies were in there, laughing at me for going with a priest to this church service.

> **"I've come to be baptized in the Holy Spirit."**

As soon as I walked into the meeting room, I was the center of attention. Everyone knew me, because I was the mayor of Warrington. I overheard comments like, "That's Charlie Osburn. Can you believe it?" and "Won't it be great if we get him?" I was never so embarrassed in my life.

Then a woman with a puzzled look on her face approached me and asked, "Why are you here?"

"I've come to be baptized in the Holy Spirit," I said.

I still don't know how those words came out of my mouth. It wasn't what I intended to say. But God was working in me, and perhaps my body wanted to follow him, even if my mind wasn't quite ready to go along.

I doubt if I'm the first person who walked into one of these meetings and asked to be baptized in the Holy Spirit. But my statement had an immediate effect. Before I knew it, I was surrounded by about 200 people. They started to pray, and one man boomed out in a loud voice, "In the name of Jesus, I command you, Satan, to get out of here."

*I have to get out of here. This is too much.* "I'm leaving," I said, and I tried to, but the circle of people was so tight that I couldn't escape. I was trapped—trapped in the Holiday Inn in the middle of a circle of fanatics who were praying about Satan. It was bad enough not to understand what was going on around me, but I couldn't figure out what was happening *inside* me, either.

> **These people have something important, and I want it.**

On the way home, I was so upset that I didn't say one word to Father Smith. But I did think about the people I had seen at these meetings. I realized that they all seemed to be truly happy. Everybody walked around with big smiles, in contrast to my constant frown.

Their joy made me realize how unhappy I was. *These people have something important, and I want it.*

When I got home, I lay down on my bed and began to cry. Then, I prayed, "Lord Jesus, if there is really anything to all this talk about the Holy Spirit, would you please give it to me? Lord Jesus, if you are really a God who comes personally into people's lives, would you become the Lord of my life? Lord Jesus, if you truly heal people, would you please heal my body?"

I had reached the bottom. I was a sick man—sick in body and sick in heart. I wept for a long time and finally fell asleep.

When I woke up the next morning, I couldn't figure out what was wrong with me. I didn't know whether to laugh or cry, to scream or sing. I began to think that I was cracking up. But I felt good, so good that I didn't care. For the first time in years, I woke up without a headache, and there was no sign of the hiatal hernia that had bothered me for eight years. I felt like a new man, physically and spiritually cleansed and reborn.

The first problem of the day came quickly. It was my turn to go to the hospital and help my wife's grandmother eat her lunch. We had never been able to get along. Sparks flew whenever we were in the same room. That morning, though, I saw a different person when I walked into the hospital room. It wasn't the same woman I had quarreled with for twenty years.

"Hello, Momsy," I said, "it's so good to see you." And I meant it.

"Get away from me," she said.

Despite her rebuff, which had come from many years of mutual disdain, I knew my heart had changed. I just wanted to hug her, but I knew this wasn't the time to try it.

■ α ■

**Suddenly, I knew that Jesus was the Lord of my life.**

■ Ω ■

After finishing at the hospital, I jumped into my car to return to the restaurant. Driving down Navy Boulevard, just three blocks from my restaurant, I passed an old Bible bookstore. Suddenly, I knew that Jesus was the Lord of my life. I knew that the God of heaven had answered the prayers of a broken man. It was as if a light had suddenly flicked on in my head. I experienced the presence of the Lord Jesus Christ in my life.

As I realized this, Jesus flooded my soul with his love. He came into my car and into my body and loved me in a way I had never experienced love before.

I eased the car over to the side of the road, and lying down on the seat, I raised my hands towards heaven. Raising my hands—something that I had disdained when I saw other people do it—no longer seemed strange. It was a natural act of submission to God, praise to the one who had forgiven my sins, healed my body, and filled my soul with a love that is impossible to describe and impossible to forget.

> **I felt like I had gone to heaven.**

I was completely overcome with gratitude. I thanked God in every way imaginable, and when my vocabulary was exhausted, I began to pray in a wonderful, strange tongue as I had heard so many other people pray. I didn't try to—it just flowed from my heart. I was praising God in his own language, worshipping him in the Spirit.

I have no idea how long I lay there praising God in tongues. I know I wanted to stay there forever. I felt the way Peter must have felt on the Mount of Transfiguration when he said, "Lord, it is good for us to be here. If you wish, I will put up three shelters . . ." (Matthew 17:4)

I felt like I had gone to heaven, and I didn't want it to end. The anger, the hatred, the depression, and the anxiety I had been carrying in my heart for years left in an instant. I felt them go. The cloud of hurt from all of the years of ambition and frustration evaporated, and a joy I had never experienced took its place.

Finally, I sat up. I was so happy; I just had to tell somebody what had happened to me. I started the engine, pulled the car around into the parking lot of the local bookstore, ran inside, and said, "I've got to tell someone what just happened to me."

A woman named Mrs. Carroll hurried out of the stock room, looked at me, and beamed. "Charlie Osburn," she said, "I'm glad to see you finally accepted Jesus into your life. Praise God! I've been praying for you for three years."

All I could do was shout, "Hallelujah! Glory to God!"

I left that store feeling like I was walking on air, a feeling that stayed with me all day.

And God had another surprise in store for me. The very moment I saw Jeanne, I saw her with spiritual eyes. *Dear God, what a wonderful wife you gave me.* I had never been able to see her spiritual beauty before. In all our years of marriage, I had looked at her only from a worldly point of view. And she usually fell short of what I thought I needed. But now, I began to see Jeanne as God wanted me to see her.

What did I see? An original masterpiece, fashioned by God's own hands. An absolute gem, revealing some of God's perfection in an earthly way. I saw her as a measure of his divine love. I fell in love with Jeanne that day, and we've had a wonderful marriage relationship ever since. We stopped building our relationship on the things of the world and built it in Jesus, instead.

> **I began to see Jeanne as God wanted me to see her.**

Of course, it took time to learn how to relate to one another in a new way. You don't change the bad habits of a lifetime in a few minutes. I had abused Jeanne for years, and I had to learn to treat her properly. Jeanne had to learn how to love me and encourage me, too. With God's help, we learned how to lay down our lives for each other the way the gospel teaches.

## Jeanne Sees Charlie Through God's Eyes

Less than three months after our twentieth wedding anniversary, on February 8, 1977, Charlie Osburn, the 'wild man of Warrington,' the man who could never change, the man that I 'had to teach a lesson to' went down on his knees with Father Smith to surrender his life to the Lord Jesus and ask for the infilling of God's Holy Spirit.

Not only was Charlie capable of changing, the Holy Spirit was up to the task of changing him. Charlie was only beginning the process of his conversion at that point, though. In time, our marriage was put in right order. It was a long, sometimes difficult process. Charlie tended to be obstinate and impulsive, and I sometimes tried to manipulate him. We had to learn how to continually forgive one another. We also had to learn how to pick ourselves up after we had fallen, then start following Jesus again.

> **We had to learn how to continually forgive one another.**

We persisted, and God continued to perform his miracles of grace and love in our lives. Charlie and I fell in love with each other all over again. On top of that, we were in love with everyone else, too!

## Charlie Learns True Forgiveness

After I committed my life to Jesus, Father Smith began to teach me about forgiveness and unconditional love. He showed me the Scriptures that commanded me to love everyone—people who had hurt me, as well as people who had been good to me.

I said, "Father Smith, are you telling me that God has forgiven everybody of their sins?"

"Yes, Charlie," he said.

"I don't believe that," I said. "There are some people that God hasn't forgiven."

"Are you sure?" he asked me.

"I'm convinced," I said.

"Name one person God doesn't love, Charlie."

"My next door neighbor," I said.

"Charlie, what did your neighbor do?"

"Father Smith, for two years, this man raped my daughter, starting at age four. He began molesting my son when he was six . . . I know God couldn't love him."

"Charlie, do you hate him?"

"Hate him? I'd like to kill him."

Father Smith sat quietly for a moment, and then asked, "Which is the greater sin—rape or murder?"

I sat there for a moment, thinking.

He repeated, "Which is the greater sin, rape or murder?"

*Murder has to be greater. You're out of here with that one.* I said, "Just maybe, murder is the greater sin."

Father Smith looked at me and said, "Charlie, you hate your neighbor?"

I said, "Father Smith, you know I do."

"Then you're a murderer."

I said, "I'm not, not, not!"

He said, "You are, are, are!"

"I didn't kill him!"

"Yes, you did"

"I did not!"

"You killed him and yourself with hate."

> "You killed him and yourself with hate."

I didn't like what Father Smith was saying to me. "Well maybe I don't hate him. I . . . just don't care for that sucker."

He went over and picked up a dictionary. He said, "Look up the word hate."

I flipped through the pages and said, "The root of hate is 'not to care for.'"

I closed the dictionary. "Father Smith, are you telling me I'm a bigger sinner than my neighbor?"

Father Smith said, "Charlie, go ask your neighbor to forgive you. You're the bigger sinner."

When I discovered all this about my neighbor, I got mad at God. I sat there and thought, *God, I don't want to do that. It was his fault. He's the culprit. He's the animal. He's the scumbag. It's not my fault. I just hate him, because of what he did.*

"Yeah," God said, "and you're the bigger sinner. Go be reconciled."

Father Smith was talking to me. I shook myself and said, "Huh?"

Father Smith said again, "Charlie, go ask your neighbor to forgive you. You're the bigger sinner."

I said, "Father Smith, are you telling me that I have to go ask *him* to forgive *me?*"

"Yes, you're the bigger sinner."

I said, "I don't think I can do that."

He said, "Then stay dead."

Everyone needs a Father Smith in their life. I wouldn't be where I am today without that wonderful brother. He's the one who brought me the Holy Spirit. He's the one who allowed me the privilege to begin to discover what God has done for me. God had mercy on me, a sinner.

Now he said, "Charlie, can you take God's mercy and extend it to someone who doesn't deserve it? That's called grace. Can you go to your neighbor and humble yourself? To be truly reconciled is to humble yourself. To humble yourself is to deny yourself. If you can humble yourself, God will exalt you."

I said, "Father Smith, I don't think I can."

For three weeks after that meeting, I walked the floor in my bedroom.

"God, I can't do it." I said.

He didn't say anything to me. He just left me alone.

I said, "God, I don't want to do it."

He didn't say a word to me.

I said, "God, I ain't going to do it."

He didn't say a word.

There's an old expression, "I'll see that guy in hell before I forgive him." I remembered Father Smith explaining what Jesus said in

Matthew 6:14–15: "For if you forgive men when they sin against you, your heavenly Father will also forgive you. But if you do not forgive men their sins, your Father will not forgive your sins." I had come to the realization that if I didn't forgive my neighbor, we would *both* end up in hell.

After three weeks, I couldn't stand it any longer. I went to the phone and called my neighbor's number at four o'clock in the morning. God had won without ever saying a word to me.

So, I called my neighbor's number. His second wife answered the phone. I couldn't remember her name, and I called her his first wife's name. I cannot tell you the words that came over that phone. The receiver kind of melted in my hand. She hung up.

> **If I didn't forgive my neighbor, we would *both* end up in hell.**

I slammed down the phone, reared back, and yelled, "God, I tried!"

I didn't know it at the time, but God had created my neighbor to help me work out my salvation. If he hadn't molested my children, I would never have found peace with God. The very thing that I was trying to push out of my life was the very thing that God wanted to use to save me.

Usually, whenever my neighbor and I passed each other, we would both look the other way. Then one day, I was backing out of my driveway with the whole family in the car. My neighbor was pulling in on his way home from work. As usual, he turned his head the other way. On this particular day, he pulled into his driveway and got out of his car. I jumped out of my car and ran up behind him.

He whirled around and put his hands up in front of his face. He said, "Don't hit me!"

I said, "Brother, I haven't come to hit you. I've come to ask you to forgive me."

My neighbor lowered his hands and looked at me in amazement.

About three months later, my neighbor approached Jeanne while she was shopping in the supermarket. This man had been out of the church for forty-five years. He had been a child abuser all of his life, because he had been abused as a child. His oldest son had just gotten out of prison for sexually abusing his own children.

My neighbor pulled a copy of the New Testament out of his pocket and said, "I've given my life to Jesus."

Jeanne said, "Praise God!"

"And I'm back in the church, going to confession, taking the sacraments, and everything."

"That's wonderful."

"I know that God has forgiven me, and I want to thank you and Charlie and your family for forgiving me, too."

> **I decided to love the man who had molested my children.**

Three weeks later, our neighbor dropped dead. Where would his soul be if I had not forgiven him? I thank God for Father Smith who taught me the importance of forgiveness while there was still time. Even though I did not have the opportunity to tell my neighbor about the Lord, my act of forgiveness prompted him to think about his own need for forgiveness. When I get to heaven, I'm going to be looking for him. I know I will live with him forever in heaven.

By the grace of God, I was given the power to make a decision about my neighbor. I decided to love the man who had molested my children, just as God loves me. I didn't preach at him or condemn him for his sin. I simply forgave him. I loved him. The result was his repentance and entry into the kingdom of God.

---

### A Prayer for the Ephesians

[14]For this reason I kneel before the Father, [15]from whom his whole family in heaven and on earth derives its name. [16]I pray that out of his glorious riches he may strengthen you with power through his Spirit in your inner being, [17]so that Christ may dwell in your hearts through faith. And I pray that you, being rooted and established in love, [18]may have power, together with all the saints, to grasp how wide and long and high and deep is the love of Christ, [19]and to know this love that surpasses knowledge—that you may be filled to the measure of all the fullness of God.

**Ephesians 3:14–19**

# CHAPTER FOUR

# Charlie, Do You Trust Me?

## Charlie Prays for a Ministry

During the days following my encounter with Jesus Christ outside the Bible bookstore, the Lord stripped the scales from my eyes. He let me see what the riches I had craved really were. They were nothing more than illusions designed by Satan to disappoint me. Everything that I had strived so hard to obtain lost its appeal to me. All I wanted to do was love my wife and my children. I wanted to begin working for the Lord.

I am not saying that everyone who has accumulated worldly wealth mishandles it the way I did. I treated money and possessions the same way I treated alcohol: I abused them. The only way I could respond was to renounce the things I couldn't control, and I am certain that this was God's desire for me.

> **The riches I had craved really were nothing more than illusions designed by Satan to disappoint me.**

I have known fine Christian people who are wealthy in the world's eyes. They have learned how to handle their wealth in a righteous way. Some of them have even become supporters of my evangelistic ministry and other ministries that build up the body of Christ.

Six months after I recommitted my life to Jesus Christ as a Catholic layman, Father Smith suggested that I enter our diocese's permanent deacon training program.

Permanent deacons are Catholic men ordained into the diaconate—the first step towards priesthood—with the understanding that they will not become ordained priests. Most permanent deacons are married men. They serve the church in a number of ways, usually by assisting parish priests. Deacons are able to do most of what a priest does, except celebrate Holy Communion or hear confessions.

Father Smith thought that the diaconate would provide a good place for me to serve, because God was clearly calling me to be a Catholic evangelist. I thought very highly of Father Smith and of his relationship with the Lord, so I agreed to apply. The screening board selected me to enter the program with about two dozen other men.

I applied myself to the studies of the training program, but most of my spiritual growth was occurring at the restaurant. As my life with God developed, I would lie awake at night and beg him to allow me to work for him. "Lord Jesus, please let me be a witness for you. Lord, give me a ministry so I can tell people about you."

> **Lord, give me a ministry so I can tell people about you.**

It wasn't long before the Lord answered that prayer. I began to witness about Jesus to every person who came in the door of my restaurant. Some people responded positively, but not everyone liked the new Charlie Osburn.

One night when I was back in the kitchen singing at the top of my lungs, Jeanne came to the door and said, "We just lost four more customers." That happened regularly.

"Glory to God!" I said. I knew who Jesus was and what he had done for me, and I couldn't keep quiet. I intended to tell the world about him, no matter what it cost me.

One day, I asked Father Smith to go on the radio and tell all the listeners what he had told me about Jesus. "I'll pay for the time," I said. "You just explain to them the love and mercy of the Lord, the same way you explained it to me."

"Charlie," he said, "I'm not comfortable doing that. I can witness one to one, but I wouldn't do well on the radio."

"Okay," I said, "If you can't do it, how about me? Will you support me if I start an evangelistic radio program for Catholics?"

"I'll do whatever I can," he said.

Not long afterward, I purchased time on a local radio station to share what I had learned about the love of Jesus. So, while I was involved in the deacon training program, I preached for thirty minutes every day on a radio show. I'd open with "Glory to God! Hallelujah! This is your Catholic lay evangelist bringing you another exciting day in the life of our Lord Jesus." I didn't know it at the time, but that radio ministry would continue for four years.

The response was great. The program was the station's biggest hit and one of the most popular radio shows in town.

One day, a woman called and said, "I tuned into your show while I was driving to the grocery store. I just couldn't turn the radio off. I sat there in the hot sun and listened until the program was over."

One evening, a couple walked in the front door of the restaurant with the biggest painting of Jesus I had ever seen.

"We've been listening to your radio program," the woman said, "The Lord told us to give this to you."

I hung the painting in the foyer of the restaurant, and under it I hung a sign that read, 'The Boss.'

Not all of my customers were pleased with that, either. My restaurant was a first-class, coat-and-tie kind of place. We catered to the rich, and the rich did not think highly of the things I was doing. That was all right with me. For years, I had tried to please and imitate the wealthy, and all it brought me was misery. It was a dead-end road. Now all I wanted was to follow Jesus and witness for him. I wanted to think like Jesus. I wanted to act like Jesus. I wanted to do the kinds of things that Jesus did.

I read the Bible every chance I got. I read the New Testament and marveled at what Jesus did. He was the only Son of the almighty God, who came to earth in obedience to his Father. He emptied himself of all that he was and took on the form of a servant. He died because he loved me—Charlie Osburn. When I understood what Jesus had done for me, I began to really study about his life. My life began to change.

> **I preached for thirty minutes every day on a radio show.**

> **I read the Bible every chance I got.**

## Jeanne Talks About Changes at the Restaurant

As things changed for Charlie, they also began to change at our restaurant, Mama Nunnari's. The first thing that changed was the ownership and the name. Charlie and I had managed the place before. We decided Jesus should manage the restaurant, so we renamed it Good News Restaurant. We decided to use it to tell everyone we met what wonderful things Jesus had done for us.

We encountered problems as soon as other Christians around town found out what we were doing. We served alcohol in our bar, and they said, "You can't possibly be Christians and love Jesus like you say you do when you are operating a bar in your restaurant."

This came as a surprise to us. We hadn't realized how strongly many Christians feel about drinking alcohol. Things were simple for us at the time. We just knew that Jesus had come in and healed our marriage. He had put a deep love in our hearts for everyone we met.

I can remember hearing Charlie on the phone one night, talking with a woman who was complaining about the bar. He didn't understand why she was upset, but he ended the conversation by saying, "Sister, if I'm doing something wrong, pray for me."

The following week, Charlie heard a radio preacher, Pastor Jackson, discussing the Letter to the Romans. The preacher read Romans 14:13: "Therefore let us stop passing judgment on one another. Instead, make up your mind not to put any stumbling block or obstacle in your brother's way."

Charlie realized that even though he differed from many Christians in his view on the righteousness of alcohol, serving alcohol in the lounge was clearly a stumbling block for some. Charlie acted immediately then, as he does now. He called and asked me to gather everyone who worked at the restaurant together for a meeting.

■ α ■
**We turned the restaurant into a Christian supper club.**
■ Ω ■

When all of our employees were assembled, Charlie looked at each person and said, "I want you to know that there will never be any kind of beverage sold in this restaurant except coffee, tea, soft drinks, and water." Then he explained why.

The bar closed, and that was the day that all but two of our employees quit. Before long, all of our regular customers also left, and we ended up with a wonderful restaurant, but no one to serve. So we turned the restaurant into a Christian supper club, which drew Christians from around town.

## Charlie Struggles to Trust God

One night, I was in the kitchen of my restaurant cooking. *If Jesus owned this restaurant, he wouldn't sell the food in it.* I looked in my Bible, and I couldn't find a single verse where it says that Jesus sold anything. When the disciples were told to set the crowd down, Jesus took fish and bread and broke it. He blessed it, and then he gave it out. He didn't tell Peter to pick up a buck-ninety-five from each person for it. He just said pick up the pieces that are left over. *Is God asking me to give away the food in my restaurant?*

And so began the process of waking up at one and two o'clock in the morning with this thought from God, "Charlie, do you trust me?"

And I would holler out, "Yes, Lord!"

"No, you don't."

"Yes, I do."

■ α ■
**"Charlie, do you trust me?"**
■ Ω ■

And this went on for two or three weeks. Then early one morning, I woke up at two o'clock. God started all over me again with this thought, "Do you really trust me?

Finally I said with a sigh, "Lord, I guess I don't."

And I didn't. I tried. I had made some effort to do it. And every time I moved towards it, I would be overwhelmed with thoughts of failure. I would think, *People will think I'm an idiot if I start giving my food away.*

You know what I was impressed with right away? God said, "They already think you're an idiot. What have you got to lose?"

I said, "How am I going to take care of the family?"

He said, "Charlie, will you trust me?"

I said, "I can't." I was right up front with him. I said, "Lord, I cannot trust you. I don't know how, but if you will teach me, I'll try."

He asked me the same question every night for a week. Finally, I said, "Lord, if I'm not trusting you, please show me where."

"I thought you gave me everything," I heard the Lord say.

"I did," I said.

"You haven't given your restaurant to me."

"Of course, I have, Lord. I even put your picture up, right there in front, where everyone can see it."

Then the Lord told me that he wanted me to give the food away, rather than sell it. He wanted me to imitate Jesus who had never sold anything, but had given away everything he had, even his very life.

"I can't run a restaurant that way, Lord." I balked at the very idea. It was easy to *say* I trusted God. But give away the food in my restaurant? It would destroy the business! I started screaming like a stuck pig.

> **α**
>
> **The Lord told me that he wanted me to give the food away.**
>
> **Ω**

I said, "Lord, your mind is against everything I've been taught. All I've ever learned is self-survival, self-protection, and self-determination. You're asking me to take you on and be a total idiot for you—a fool for Christ."

He said, "Now you're getting closer."

God wanted to strip away the thing that had been my god all my life—my money. It hurt like the dickens.

One night while I was in the kitchen, I was thinking and praying in tongues. Suddenly, I had this tremendous insight on the whole universe. In my mind, I was able to see the entire universe, particularly the colors. I was not hallucinating on drugs. In this frame of mind—in a wonderful spirit of ecstasy—God spoke to me.

He said, "There is one god who made everything and another one who is trying to destroy everything." This wonderful voice inside said, "Charlie, I had you in mind when I made all of this."

All of a sudden, I had the thought that I believe in one God, the Father. In an instant, I realized that I had never asked to be brought into this world. Someone had to pick me. There has never been anyone else in this world like me, and there never will be another. I was a unique creation of God. Everything he has ever made is unique. All of a sudden, God became my father. The most marvelous experience I ever had was in understanding that God was really my father. He formed me before the foundation of this world. He had me in his heart, his mind, his hand before all of creation was made.

God really impressed something on me that evening. He said, "Charlie, don't you think I could run this restaurant? Don't you think I am in charge of everything already? Don't you know that I'm the boss?"

The next day, I took my menu to a printer and asked him to print it again, but without the prices.

"What for?" he asked. "Are you going to change the prices every day?"

"No," I said, "God's telling me to give my food away."

"What?" he said. "Charlie, you're crazy. You can't do this."

I had a tough time with the printer. He didn't want to do it, because he thought I was losing my mind. I thought he might be right. Losing money was not my idea of fun. But God had told me that he would take care of me.

The printer persisted. "Charlie, you just can't do this."

"I have no choice," I answered. "Jesus Christ has become Lord of my life. I have surrendered everything to him. I know people will think I'm a fool, but I'd rather be a fool for Jesus than successful in this world."

In the end, the printer gave in and printed the menu without prices.

I felt as though I were hanging over the edge of a cliff the day I put those new menus into my customers' hands. I knew that Jesus was in charge. I also knew that the people coming in to dine could take advantage of me. I had never in all my life been in that position.

> **The printer printed the menu without prices.**

This began quite a stir among the people in the deacon training program, in my parish, and among my friends and neighbors. They could not understand why I would do such a thing. One day in church, I was even the subject of a sermon, in which the priest accused me of being on an ego trip.

All this came as quite a shock to me, because I thought I was only doing what Jesus wanted. The greatest shock came at a meeting that Jeanne and I had with the director of the diaconate program. We had been meeting with him regularly so that he could evaluate my progress. And since Jeanne and I spent most of our time at the restaurant, we always met there.

The director came in, and we all sat down around a table. He looked at me and said, "Charlie, you're turning people off with your preaching. We can't attract any new men to the diaconate program, because you're scaring them away."

> **"You've got to stop turning people off."**

I was stunned! Were people actually not entering the diaconate simply because I was in it?

The director said, "Charlie, I want you to slow down here. You're going too fast. You've got to stop turning people off."

Ever since I had given my life to Jesus and experienced the baptism in the Holy Spirit, I wanted to share it. I had experienced the wonderful love of Jesus, and I wanted to share it. Why shouldn't everyone experience the joy of the Lord? If the Lord would give to me, he'd give himself to anyone. I knew that was the message God wanted me to share with people.

Now, I happen to be an exuberant man. I like to shout. So when Jesus came into my life and filled me with his joy, I began shouting, "Glory! Hallelujah!" everywhere I went.

I had received positive calls from radio listeners about my ministry. People in the restaurant responded to me. So when the director of the diaconate told me I was turning people off, it was a real blow. I didn't want to turn people off. I wanted to turn them on to Jesus and show them his love.

Shortly after our meeting ended, I became physically ill and went home to bed. The next morning, I went to the restaurant, but after an hour, I went home sick again. I had never been this ill in my life.

I prayed all afternoon. "Lord, what am I going to do? Show me what to do."

At about five o'clock in the afternoon, I went back to the restaurant. The first thing I noticed as I walked in the door, was a piece of blue paper on the counter. I picked it up and saw that it was addressed to me. I was so dejected that I just stuck it in my pocket and sat down at a table. After a while, I pulled the note out of my pocket and read it. It had been written by a lady in the prayer group that Jeanne and I attended. What I read was an amazing answer to the anguished prayers I had prayed all day long.

The note read, "Dear Charles, I've been meaning to tell you this for a long time. You cannot turn off those that are turned on. And those that are turned off have already turned away."

> ■ α ■
> **I couldn't turn people off—they turn themselves off.**
> ■ Ω ■

*That's it! That's the answer.* I realized that if you turn off a light switch and hold it down for fifty years, the lights will never be more turned off than they were when you depressed the switch. When they're off, they're off. But if you move your finger and put a little pressure in the opposite direction, you can turn the lights on.

I knew then that I could not turn someone off. No evangelist can. I couldn't turn people off—they turn themselves off. But if we talk and preach long enough, some of those who have been turned off will make the choice to turn themselves back on. They will receive the light of Jesus into their lives and know the same joy that I do.

Even though I couldn't turn people off, I realized, I could anger them. I had upset quite a few apple carts. But so did Jesus, and so did the apostle Paul. They were both driven out of several towns. But there were always a few people who followed them, because they had been turned back on. They believed the message of love and received the joy of the Lord into their lives.

I didn't want to alienate anyone, so I made a sincere effort to follow the directives laid down for me by the director of the diaconate program. I had to. God had placed him in a position of authority over me, and God expected me to obey him.

I finished the deacon training for the diaconate. Jeanne and I went to see the bishop to decide whether or not I should be ordained as a permanent deacon. Bishop Lorenzo told us that he didn't think I should be ordained. He told me later that there was a look of shock on my face, followed almost instantly by a look of relief and peace. He believed that God could use me better as a lay evangelist. Jeanne and I agreed, so I withdrew from the program.

> **My new patrons were alcoholics, prostitutes, and street people.**

My price-free menu quickly drove away the last of my rich customers, and the restaurant began to fill up with the poor. The word got around that there was a crazy man down on Navy Boulevard giving away his food. My new patrons were alcoholics, prostitutes, and street people of all kinds. These were the poor whom society had rejected—the ones the world had no place for. Now, they had a place where they could break bread.

At first, I was thrilled with this development. God was using my restaurant to reach society's outcasts. However, when the thrill wore off, my old fears returned.

When I began to give away food in my restaurant, I thought everybody would appreciate it. It was the biggest joke in town. I became the laughingstock of Pensacola, Florida. When people began to come in, eat, and then walk out while laughing at me, I got angry about it.

> **I became the laughingstock of Pensacola.**

I said, "Lord, people are laughing at me."
He said, "Welcome to the club."
"You know," I said, "I don't like this."
He said, "I didn't either."

I said, "They're abusing a privilege."

He said, "I know."

I said, "I don't like this one bit."

I was really upset. You know what I discovered? I was selfish. God began to pull this long rope of selfishness out of my heart.

I said, "You've got it all."

And God said, "No, I haven't even started yet."

"God, what are you doing?" I asked one night when a scantily clad girl came in. She was wearing short-shorts, a T-shirt, and nothing else. She came in drunk with six other people and sat down at a table in the middle of the restaurant. They ate so much, I wondered where on earth they were putting it.

I knew those people weren't going to give me a cent, even though they were eating a mountain of food. We had cut a hole in the counter where the cash register had been and posted a sign welcoming donations for the ministry.

> ■ α ■
> "What are you doing, Lord?"
> ■ Ω ■

After three months, we hadn't received any money at all. We were rapidly running out of money and out of food in the pantry. I began to panic.

"What are you doing, Lord?" I asked. I stood there in my restaurant with tears coming to my eyes. "I'm running out of everything—money, food, everything. I won't be able to continue doing what you told me to do. I can't give away food if I don't have money to buy it with in the first place."

"Charlie, do you trust me?" was all I could hear the Lord saying.

"I have nothing to trust you with," I said.

"Good," the Lord said. "Now you can really begin to trust me."

---

**Treasures in Heaven**

[19]"Do not store up for yourselves treasures on earth, where moth and rust destroy, and where thieves break in and steal. [20]But store up for yourselves treasures in heaven, where moth and rust do not destroy, and where thieves do not break in and steal. [21]For where your treasure is, there your heart will be also.

**Matthew 6:19–21**

CHAPTER FIVE

# Lord, What Are You Doing to Us?

## Charlie Overcomes Anger with Love

I couldn't stand watching those kids, those drunks and addicts take away every last thing that I had worked so hard to obtain. So I decided to go over to that table and run them off. I just about flew out of the kitchen, I was so angry.

"Lord," I said, "I can't take it. Out they go."

"Don't you dare touch one of mine," he said.

I arrived at the table, my Bible in hand, with God's warning ringing in my ears. The street kids looked up at me with curiosity.

I slammed my Bible down as hard as I could. "I've come to tell you about Jesus," I said.

"Okay," one of them said. "We've never really heard much about Jesus. We'd like to hear about him."

"What? You would?"

The Lord had turned my anger and frustration inside out so that I would share his gospel with some young people who really needed to hear it. Each of those young people agreed that night to think about committing their lives to Jesus. Several of them said a prayer of commitment with me, and they were sincere. They had heard about God before, but they had not received the good news like they did that night. Right there in my restaurant, God healed them from sicknesses, delivered them from drugs, and showed them the depth of his love. It was one of the most wonderful experiences of my life.

Two weeks later, the young woman who had been drunk that night came back to the restaurant. She was wearing a nice dress, and the gaudy makeup was gone. She looked very pretty. She came in and asked me to read more Scriptures to her.

I don't know what happened to the others. I never saw them again. I hope that they found a body of Christians so they could grow in the Christian life. That's what I encouraged them to do.

You know what God taught me through that experience? He taught me how selfish I had been. I never knew I was so selfish until people began to come in and take advantage of me. They wouldn't even say thank you. You know those 5,000 people that Jesus fed? I've never read where they said thank you to Jesus, either. So when you start walking this walk, don't expect people to come back and thank you. They may not even remember your name. But Jesus will.

That episode was a turning point in my life. I became totally consumed with the thought of trying to be like Jesus. In making an attempt to be like Jesus, I began to love people. I never again wanted to have a part in selling anything, because the minute a person might become less important than a piece of cake that sells for $3.95, I could lose my respect and admiration for them.

God began to teach me how to love his people. I learned it was the poor, the neglected, and the humble who were most interested in hearing about God's love. Most of my customers from the old days were not. They weren't interested in anything that was free, and they weren't interested in hearing about Jesus.

> **God began to teach me how to love his people.**

When I approached a wealthy customer and said, "Brother, there's more to life than that bottle of wine," the response was usually, "Leave me alone, Charlie. I'm paying a good price for this meal."

I just couldn't stop talking about the Lord. I felt that he wanted me to share the Good News with everyone I came in contact with, so I kept trying. Looking back, I have to admit that it was no way to run a restaurant. Within about a year, I had run off most of my original clientele. I was still convinced, though, that I was doing what God wanted me to do.

## Jeanne Tries to Keep the Peace at Home

Now these two Osburns, who were in love with each other and on fire for Jesus, had five other Osburns in the house with a different point of view. We had taught our five children how to live well in the world. We had taught them how to make it on their own, how to watch out for 'number one,' and how to party. They knew how to survive in the world, but suddenly, their parents started living like Christians, putting Jesus first. That was contrary to everything we had taught them.

> **Their parents started living like Christians, putting Jesus first.**

The three oldest ones scattered. Our oldest son, Brian, got married and joined the Air Force, both on the same day. Our daughter, Regina, was already married by then. Our second son, Craig, moved out and got married a short while later.

Suddenly, we found ourselves with only two children at home, Doug and Amy. Doug was the most rebellious child I had ever seen. He was so full of resentment that he wouldn't even speak to anyone else in the house. He just walked past us as fast as he could without saying a word.

One night, Charlie was out speaking to a prayer group. He called me afterward. "Honey," he said in an excited voice, "Praise the Lord! How are things going?"

*Do you really want to know how things are going back here?* I kept my thoughts to myself and told him about a few other things.

"What's wrong with you?" he asked "I don't hear that joy in your voice."

I told him all about Doug.

Charlie said, "I want you to love Doug just the way he is. Don't expect him to do anything for you."

The next evening, Doug came to me and asked for two dollars. I had two dollars, but that was all I had. I didn't respond immediately, because I was busy washing the evening dishes. I then forgot all about my son's request and left the house with my daughter, Amy.

I had been driving for about fifteen minutes when I remembered that I had not given Doug the two dollars. As I turned the car around, Amy said, "Mom, you're not really driving all the way back home just to give Doug two dollars, are you?"

"I sure am," I said, hurrying back home.

As I pulled into the carport, Doug shoved open the back door and walked past us, saying, "It's too late. I don't want your money any more."

I could sense what Amy was thinking. She wanted to strike out at her ungrateful brother. Still smiling, I put the car in reverse, and pulled out into the street. I said to Amy, "We have to love Doug the way he is."

The next morning, Doug passed me in the hall.

"Doug," I said, "your two dollars are on the kitchen counter. Please forgive me for the resentment I had in my heart for you last night."

That evening, as I was coming out of my bedroom, Doug met me in the hallway. He leaned over and kissed me on the cheek. "Mom," he said, "I want you to know how much I love you."

> I had to die to myself and reach out to love him with God's love.

That was the beginning of a new and open relationship between Doug and me. There has been no more rebellion, no more resentment. But it came at a high cost. I had to die to myself and reach out to love him with God's love.

Amy, who was twelve years old when Jesus came into our home, also changed a great deal. She was accustomed to getting whatever she wanted, whenever she wanted it. We had raised her that way. Then, she changed right along with us. Because of the changes at the restaurant, we didn't have reliable income. We no longer had the money to get her everything she wanted, although, for the first time in her life, we were able to give her all the love she wanted and needed.

One day, she came to me and said, "Mom, I know you don't have the money for this. But do you suppose that if I asked Jesus, he would send us some money so I can get a pair of shoes? I really need them."

It was all I could do to keep from bursting into tears.

Our little girl had been hurt deeply in her life, but God had healed her. Her simple, childlike request really touched me. We prayed right there, and in a few days, she was able to get the new shoes she needed.

As Charlie and I learned how to take seriously the words of the gospel and the teachings of the Catholic Church, our children and other relatives saw our sincerity and our dedication and responded to it. Time and again, we asked each of our children to forgive us for the mistakes we had made and for the many times we had failed to love them and care adequately for their needs. The healing took years, and, in fact, is still going on. But God continues to be faithful.

## Charlie Puts Jesus in Charge

After Jeanne and I put Jesus in charge of the restaurant, a lot of people thought I had gone overboard. But I don't think you can ever go overboard for Jesus. Wherever Jesus went, he caused a commotion, and so did the apostle Paul. Paul caused riots in city after city. In John 15:18, Jesus said, "If the world hates you, keep in mind that it hated me first."

> **We asked each of our children to forgive us for the mistakes we had made.**

Every morning, I'd show up early at the restaurant, and there would be maybe 100 pounds of potatoes, 2,000 pounds of shrimp, and big piles of bread at the back door.

I would say, "Lord you've done it again. You send it, and I'll give it away." You know, I did that for two years. I never did run out of food. I ran out of reputation, though. My reputation got ruined in a hurry, because I had taken a restaurant that had been a landmark in Pensacola, and it turned out to be a bumhole.

After all my regular customers stopped coming and all my resources were gone, the Lord showed me that it was the needy people—the drug addicts, the prostitutes, the poor, and the neglected—who were the ones who would open their hearts to God.

They would go to Jeanne, asking for help. One girl told Jeanne that she wanted to find a respectable job. "I can't go back to the nightclub and sell myself to men anymore," she said.

So we helped them find jobs and break out of bad relationships. We helped them find the Lord.

> **The Lord showed me that it was the needy people who would open their hearts to God.**

## Jeanne Prays for the Ability to Love Others

When the Lord led Charlie to take the prices off the menu, the Christians stopped coming. They found it too confusing to have to figure out how much to pay for their food.

During all this time of trying to live the gospel, there was one great woman who stood quietly in the background, praying with all her might. That woman was my mother, Janet Nunnari.

Mama and her brothers had operated a number of restaurants in the Pensacola area for decades. In fact, Charlie and I got into the restaurant business because of their success. We took the business over from them, and even though we changed it quite a bit, we probably would not have been successful if it hadn't been for their reputation and my mother's ability to cook.

During all our years of troubled marriage, Mama stood by us. She was our chief cook, and she never missed a day. Even after Charlie took the prices off the menus, she stayed with us, cooking for the down-and-out people and watching forty years of hard work in the restaurant business go down the drain. When we stopped paying our employees, Mama continued to work, happy to do so.

Papa also helped with the restaurant. He got up very early every morning to drive Mama to pick up the supplies she needed for the day. Then, he dug through the dumpster out back to make sure none of the dish washers or wait staff had thrown away the silverware. Charlie said that Papa was the most Christ-like person he had ever met. He never said a bad word about anybody, and he never complained. I think he had the greatest impact on Charlie as he was growing as a Christian.

> **Charlie and I were able to grow because of my parents' faithfulness and prayers.**

I believe that Charlie and I were able to grow as quickly as we did because of my parents' faithfulness to us and because of their prayers. Many times, it was very hard for them to watch what was happening. But they kept quiet, prayed for us, and supported us as best they could. They were the most positive people we have ever known. They never said a bad word about anyone. Their love was rewarded. They saw our family turned around, and they saw the fruit of evangelization that went on in the Good News Restaurant. That was enough for them. They were very happy for us.

Eventually, the only people who came to the restaurant were street people. We were living out the Scripture from Luke 6:34–35:

> And if you lend to those from whom you expect repayment, what credit is that to you? Even 'sinners' lend to 'sinners,' expecting to

be repaid in full. But love your enemies, do good to them, and lend to them without expecting to get anything back. Then your reward will be great, and you will be sons of the Most High, because he is kind to the ungrateful and wicked.

Not long after we made this change, the doors of the restaurant swung open, and a man stuck his head in.

"Lady," he said to me, "is this the place where you can come and get a steak for a quarter?"

*Oh, Lord! What are you doing to us?* I thought.

That night, Charlie was so upset that he went into the men's restroom and cried out, "Oh, God, help me!"

At the same time, I was in the ladies' room saying, "Jesus, what are you doing?"

Charlie and I soon realized how helpless we were. We still held onto the things we had accumulated, and that selfishness was hard to let go of. The whole process of letting go was very uncomfortable, but we learned an important lesson. The Lord showed us that we were supposed to love the poor, the weak, and the neglected. We were supposed to love them right into the kingdom of God. If they were going to be evangelized, and if they were ever going to discover that they were sons and daughters of the living God, they had to experience love from us so that they could recognize God's love when he showed it to them.

> **Selfishness was hard to let go of.**

A couple—Shirley and her boyfriend—used to come in frequently, and God used them to show me where my heart was. They were always on drugs or alcohol. They ordered the best dinners on the menu. Every time they came in, our waitress, Hilda Wheelis, would tell them about the Lord, but it didn't seem to sink in.

One night, as I watched them walk across the parking lot towards the front door, I said, "Lord, no. Not them again. I can't take this anymore." I put my head down on the counter and said, "Lord, you are going to have to give me your love, because I have no more love to give."

One evening, Charlie said that the Lord wanted him to go out among the customers and share about Jesus. He invited those who wanted Jesus to be the Lord of their lives to come and pray with him. One of the first ones up was Shirley. She stood next to Charlie, with a big smile on her face, and she gave him a kiss. Then a young man came forward while I was playing the piano. He looked familiar, but I didn't recognize him. Then I looked into his eyes and realized it was Shirley's boyfriend. He had had hair down to his waist, and he had always worn a big old marijuana belt buckle. That night, he was dressed well, and his hair was cut shorter than Charlie's. Both Shelia and her friend surrendered their lives to the Lord that night. God allowed me to witness it. He had truly answered my prayers!

Months later, Shirley came up to me and said, "Jeanne, can I say a prayer with you?"

"Of course, Shirley."

She reached for my hand and prayed, "Father, I want to thank you for Charlie and Jeanne loving me, when I didn't know you even existed."

## Charlie Remembers Hilda Wheelis

We were thankful to God for the people who came into our lives, too. Their help in the restaurant was invaluable, because the only employees who remained were my mother-in-law—one of the best professional cooks in that part of Florida—and a very special waitress named Hilda Wheelis. I first got to know Hilda when she filled in from time to time for one of her daughters who was a waitress in my restaurant. Hilda knew all about my conversion to Christ, and when I dedicated the restaurant to the Lord, she came to work for me full-time.

After all the other employees had left, Hilda came to me and said, "If you can give away your food, I can give away my time."

**"If you can give away your food, I can give away my time."**

Hilda was totally committed to the Lord. Why? Because she had found out firsthand what a good God he is.

A few years before I met Hilda, she had been a very sick woman. She had had stomach ulcers, colitis, arthritis, deterioration of the bones, and a blood disease — all at the same time. She was put on a special diet to control the ulcers, but the food on that diet aggravated the colitis. The doctors prescribed aspirin for the arthritis, which then aggravated the ulcers. What's more, the bone condition was incurable, and the blood disease was not responding to treatment. Hilda had been in and out of a number of hospitals for several years, until the doctors finally gave up. They told her that she had reached the point of no return and that she would soon become completely incapacitated.

Fortunately, Hilda had a friend who insisted that she attend a healing service conducted by a Catholic priest, Father Tobias. Hilda didn't believe in healing, but her friend persisted, so Hilda agreed to go. The service was in Mobile, Alabama, and the van they took to get there had improperly installed seats which aggravated Hilda's condition. By the time she arrived in Mobile, Hilda was in agony.

Hilda's friend helped her to the church, and they took seats near the back. Hilda heard little of what Father Tobias was saying, because she was in so much pain. After he finished his talk, however, she did hear him say that he was going to pray with every person present, beginning with those in pain. Hilda still did not believe in faith healing, but she raised her hand when he asked who was in pain at that moment.

When Father Tobias went to pray with Hilda, he surprised her by telling her several things about her life that he simply could not have known had the Holy Spirit not revealed them to him. This is a spiritual gift which is sometimes called 'revelation' or 'word of knowledge.' It is like the gift of prophecy, where someone speaks to another on behalf of God.

These personal revelations concerned things in Hilda's life that were causing her great emotional pain. Father Tobias told her that unless she forgave the people who were hurting her—including her own husband who was living with another woman—she would never get well. He helped her understand that forgiveness is a decision, not a feeling. Hilda asked the Lord for the grace to decide to forgive her husband. Then Father Tobias prayed with her, and the pain immediately left her body. God had healed her completely.

During the next few days, Hilda began to try foods that she had been unable to eat for years. To her surprise, she could eat them without pain.

**Forgiveness is a decision, not a feeling.**

Later, when she returned to her doctor for tests that had been scheduled prior to the healing service, he told her to stop taking her medications. He could find no symptoms of her diseases.

As you might expect, Hilda was overjoyed at her healing and returned to the sessions conducted by Father Tobias to learn more about the Lord. Eventually, she told the Lord that she wanted to serve him in whatever way he wanted. She began going downtown every day after work to tell prostitutes, homosexuals, and others about the healing power of Jesus.

Knowing very well what God could do for needy people, Hilda soon became a prayer warrior around the restaurant. When she prayed with people, they were healed. She had strong faith and a big heart filled with love.

Jeanne and I leaned heavily on Hilda during the three months after all our employees left us. It was an ordeal, and she was a pillar of strength for us. We ran out of just about everything, and people said terrible things about us. But as we started sharing Jesus with those who wanted him most, God began to show us how he was upholding us.

At the end of those three months, more than one hundred people were working at the restaurant. Most of them had come in off the street, looking for a handout. Instead, they met Jesus Christ. They worked without pay and did just about everything. In fact, I hardly had to work myself. So I preached.

---

**Jesus Heals a Paralytic**
[1] Jesus stepped into a boat, crossed over and came to his own town. [2] Some men brought to him a paralytic, lying on a mat. When Jesus saw their faith, he said to the paralytic, "Take heart, son; your sins are forgiven."

[3] At this, some of the teachers of the law said to themselves, "This fellow is blaspheming!"

[4] Knowing their thoughts, Jesus said, "Why do you entertain evil thoughts in your hearts? [5] Which is easier: to say, 'Your sins are forgiven,' or to say, 'Get up and walk'? [6] But so that you may know that the Son of Man has authority on earth to forgive sins. . . ." Then he said to the paralytic, "Get up, take your mat and go home." [7] And the man got up and went home. [8] When the crowd saw this, they were filled with awe; and they praised God, who had given such authority to men.

**Matthew 9:1–8**

CHAPTER SIX

# My Mission in Life

## Charlie Feeds the Poor

It seems that there is a special relationship between food and Jesus. Jesus is the spiritual food we all so greatly need. I learned to take advantage of that relationship between Jesus and food.

I would take the microphone while my patrons were eating and say, "Dear brothers and sisters, I want to thank the one who allowed this meal to be possible for you. His name is Jesus."

Everyone would clap.

Then I would ask, "Is there anyone here tonight who wants to give his life to Jesus?"

Sometimes only a few people would pray with me, but at other times, table after table of men and women would stand up and join me in a prayer of surrender to the Lord.

Many of the people who responded to my preaching were Catholics. I began to see ever more clearly that my mission in life was to win souls for the Lord as a Catholic evangelist. In fact, I believe that is the mission of every Catholic—indeed, every Christian. As far as I am concerned, that is why we are on earth. We have been created, baptized, and blessed in abundance so we can win souls for the kingdom of our Lord Jesus Christ. The money we've made, the things we've done as artists, craftsmen, writers, or anything else won't matter when we get to heaven. What God is interested in is whether we have given his love to others.

> **My mission in life was to win souls for the Lord as a Catholic evangelist.**

When Jesus was asked which was the greatest commandment in the Law, he replied in Matthew 22:37–39, "'Love the Lord your God with all your heart and with all your soul and with all your mind.' This is the first and greatest commandment. And the second is like it: 'Love your neighbor as yourself.'" At judgment, God is going to ask me a question: "Did you reach out to the poor, the hungry, the naked, and the lonely with my love? What did you do to feed their empty stomachs and their empty spirits? Did you tell others about how I could help them?"

How will I answer?

It liberated me to discover what God thinks is important. I found that money, success, and what people thought of me didn't matter at all. I was excited about serving the Lord. I would get up in the morning, jumping with joy, and I'd go to bed at night in the same way. Winning souls for the Lord is the most thrilling thing we can do.

I believed so much in this ministry to the needy that, after closing the lounge, I had the bar ripped out and turned the room into a dormitory for homeless men. We installed a shower and put in sixteen cots. Some nights, there were more men than cots, so we'd bring the extras home. Many times, Jeanne would pin a note to the back door, telling our children to be careful where they walked when they came in the house. We didn't want them to step on a man in a sleeping bag on the dining room floor.

Each morning, I conducted a Bible study for these men and prayed with those who were interested. Then, they'd work around the restaurant or go out and look for jobs. Our shelter became well known. Sometimes, the sheriff's deputies would stop by with a carload of drifters to drop them off for a couple of hot meals and a good night's sleep.

One Sunday morning when Jeanne and I arrived at the restaurant, we saw a beat-up old station wagon parked out front. Inside were three ragged men.

One of them said, "The cops told us to come here. They told us you'd give us something to eat. They said you'd take care of us."

One of these guys was a huge man, the biggest man I had ever seen. He owned nothing but the clothes on his back, and they weren't in very good shape. We had clothing available for people who needed it, but we had nothing that would fit this man. So Jeanne called up a seamstress we knew and asked her to make this fellow some clothes.

A few nights later, I woke up in the middle of the night and began to pray. While I was talking with the Lord, he told me to give our car to our large friend. I woke up Jeanne to tell her this news.

"Praise the Lord," she said. She admitted later that she didn't really mean it.

The next morning, I told the man that God wanted me to give him our car. He said that he couldn't accept it, and I was relieved. I really didn't want to give away our only car.

Then, one morning while Jeanne and I were praying, we were both overcome with the conviction that we had to give up the car. The issue wasn't the car itself, but our desire to cling to this possession, rather than the Lord. We hurried over to the restaurant and told our big friend that God really wanted us to give him our car.

> ■ α ■
> **God really wanted us to give him our car.**
> ■ Ω ■

He was doing some work in the parking lot when we spoke with him. He said, "No one has ever given me anything in my entire life." He fell down on the pavement and began to cry.

He never did accept the car, but he did come to believe in the Lord and began to live like a Christian. He stayed with us for several weeks and then left. He continued to drift around the area, but with a new purpose. Instead of stealing to earn his livelihood, he found odd jobs and used most of the money he earned to repay people he had stolen from in the past. He kept in touch with us, assuring us that he was getting his life together, with the help of the Lord.

Months went by. Our work for the Lord was thrilling, but it was also hard work. We'd work in the restaurant eighteen hours a day, feeding hungry people and ministering to everyone who was interested in Jesus Christ. Jeanne and I would drag ourselves out of the restaurant at one o'clock in the morning, absolutely exhausted, and walk home hand in hand. We had eventually given up our car, so we had to walk everywhere. But we were happy, and we'd sing Christian songs on the way home.

I had bad days, too. Every day, people came into the restaurant just to take advantage of the free food. I sometimes got upset with the Lord and cried out, "They're taking advantage of me!"

He said, "They took advantage of me, too. Are you any better than I am?"

"But, Lord, they're ripping me off."

"They ripped me off, too."

"They're making fun of me."

"They made fun of me, too. They ridiculed me, Charlie, in ways they can never ridicule you."

"I know, Lord, but it hurts. Lord, it hurts."

Then the Lord would send in a whole gang of people who were drunk or high on drugs and say, "Charlie, if you can't love them, then you don't love me."

I knew I wanted to love the Lord. I said, "Lord, teach me to love them. I have to know how to love these people. If that's what's required of me, I have to learn how."

> **God gave me the grace to witness to them about his love and mercy.**

And every time I prayed for it, God gave me the grace, not only to feed them gladly, but to witness to them about his love and mercy.

After two years of evangelizing, speaking on the radio, giving away food at the restaurant, and housing homeless men, I began speaking more often to Christian groups in other states. As I traveled more, Jeanne found it increasingly difficult to manage the restaurant by herself.

One day when I returned from a trip, we talked about this problem. I knew that I had to make a choice. If the Lord was calling me to preach, I would have to close the restaurant. I found it impossible to choose between the two. So, I decided to leave it up to the Lord.

"Jeanne," I said, "next weekend, I'll be out of town. You operate the restaurant as usual. If no one shows up on Sunday, we'll shut her down."

Normally, Sunday was our busiest day of the week. But on that Sunday in September of 1979, a huge storm moved in from the Gulf of Mexico. Fourteen inches of rain fell on Pensacola, and everything was flooded. It was impossible to drive, or even walk outdoors. Not one person came to the restaurant.

When I heard the news on TV, I called Jeanne. "When you leave tonight," I told her, "lock the place up tight. We're closing."

# CHAPTER SEVEN

# Walking in Faith

## Charlie Discovers That Blessings Follow Faith

After we closed the restaurant, we walked in faith every day, and the Lord came through. We didn't starve. We didn't even suffer. In fact, in many ways we grew and prospered. Jeanne and I grew closer together, and we spent more time with our children. We no longer felt pressured by the demands of the restaurant, so we had more time to pray, study the Scriptures, and share the good news with people in hospitals and nursing homes.

After I spoke at a few Catholic prayer meetings in northern Florida, other invitations began to come in. I spoke at a number of meetings of the Full Gospel Businessmen's Fellowship and at many Protestant churches. The more I spoke, the more I wanted to know about where God was leading me.

Before my conversion, all I knew about authority was what I had learned through my business. I had thirty-two employees under my authority. I told them to be at work at a certain time, and they were there. When I told them to go home, they went. They were under my authority, and they obeyed.

Scripture clearly says that God has put us all under authority. As Catholics, we are under the authority of our bishops. Therefore, I wanted to know what they wanted me to do as a Catholic layman. I had already discovered who I was in Jesus. Now, I needed to know how I fit into the body of Christ. I had already spoken with my pastor and read things that my own bishop had written.

> ■ α ■
> **I needed to know how I fit into the body of Christ.**
> ■ Ω ■

But I had no idea that the bishops of the Catholic Church had written a document describing precisely what they expected of me.

I was in San Antonio, Texas, one night, presenting the story of my conversion at some Catholic prayer meetings. After one of the meetings, a leader of one of the prayer groups handed me a thick document.

"Charlie," he said, "you have to read this."

"No," I said, "it's too thick."

"Look," he said, I've already got it underlined for you. Just read the parts I've marked."

I looked at what he had underlined. "I guess that won't be so hard," I said. "What is this?"

"A copy of what 2,500 bishops who met in Rome for a council have to say about us—the church. I've highlighted the parts about the Decree on the Apostolate of Lay People."

I started reading that night. I discovered that the bishops weren't just talking to each other. They weren't just talking to the priests and nuns. They were talking to me, Charlie Osburn, a layman. The bishops wrote that lay people have a share of Jesus' ministry. We are all priests, prophets, and kings. We have an assignment—a mission—to bring other men and women to Jesus Christ and his church. That's a big job and a big responsibility. And I had never heard that I was supposed to be part of it. This part of the bishops' message from the Decree on the Apostolate of Lay People really stood out in my mind:

> ■ α ■
> **We have an assignment—a mission—to bring other men and women to Jesus Christ and his church.**
> ■ Ω ■

> The council, then, makes to all the laity an earnest appeal in the Lord to give a willing, noble and enthusiastic response to the voice of Christ, who at this hour is summoning them more pressingly, and to the urging of the Holy Spirit. It is the Lord himself, by this council, who is once more inviting all the laity to unite themselves to him ever more intimately, to consider his interests their own, and to join in his mission as savior. It is the Lord who is again sending them into every town and every place where he himself is to come. He sends them on the church's apostolate . . . where they are to show themselves his cooperators, doing their full share continually in the work of the Lord, knowing that in the Lord their labor cannot be lost.

As I was reading, I felt as though I had had my sight restored. St. Paul received back his physical sight, but more importantly, he received spiritual vision. The Lord told him what to do. Now, through the bishops' decree, the Lord had shown me what to do.

For most of my life, I had sought to be famous in the world, never realizing what my place in it was meant to be. The council document opened up a whole new world to me. I realized that I didn't have to be a mayor, a successful businessman, or anything else to be happy and fulfilled in life.

I had been baptized into the church. I was called to be an apostle of Jesus Christ and to cooperate with him. I was anointed—filled with the Holy Spirit—so I could preach the gospel of Jesus.

I realized that this was not just true for me. It was true for all people. We are all supposed to spread the gospel of Jesus Christ.

The bishops also clearly said that God himself assigns to each person a practical role in the church's mission of spreading the kingdom of God throughout the world. Furthermore, if we aren't involved in apostolic work that helps the church grow by evangelizing new members and by sanctifying current members, we are useless. That means we are useless to the church *and* to ourselves. Jesus warns us in Matthew 7:19, "Every tree that does not bear good fruit is cut down and thrown in the fire."

> **If we aren't involved in apostolic work we are useless.**

I found out as I continued reading the bishops' decree that we can be useful, because God gives us the spiritual gifts we need in our ministry. I thought *if God is equipping us, what more do we need?* Yet, I noticed that the lay people in a typical Catholic parish on Sunday mornings acted as if God hadn't done anything to prepare them.

I was excited to learn that, through the bishops of the Second Vatican Council, God was telling all of us how to live a life of Christian service. The Decree on the Apostolate of Lay People tells us who we are, what the Lord and the church expect of us, how we fit into the body, and how we should exercise our gifts and talents. I saw that it was, very simply, a complete course in Christian living. I wanted to tell everyone, "Read it! Study it! Apply it, and your everyday Christian life will take off like a rocket."

> **God gives us the spiritual gifts we need in our ministry.**

God revealed to me that anger, judgment, and condemnation were not the best ways to respond to our world's problems. He showed me that one reason the world is in the state it's in is because we Christians are not doing our jobs.

I had been a lover of things and a user of people. I was not loving, evangelizing, or serving. With God's grace, I wanted to be a user of things and a lover of people. I was ready to have an intimate, everyday relationship with Jesus and view everything that happened in my life as an opportunity to witness to someone about his love. And I wanted to encourage every person I met to do the same.

What could be more exciting than to encourage Catholic lay people—men and women, boys and girls—to take on this opportunity to evangelize the world? I knew that they needed someone to tell them that they had a choice to make. They could choose to be part of Jesus' work, or ignore it. They could sit back and leave the church's work to the priests and nuns. I wanted to tell people that they were missing out on great blessings by waiting for someone else to do their work.

I felt God calling me to tell the world a very important message. We can only do this work when we know that we are sons and daughters of the living God, that we have a glorious reward in heaven, and that we're going to get there by doing the work Jesus wants us to do.

It was tremendously exciting to discover who I was, where I came from, and where I was going. With that knowledge, I felt bolder than I had ever felt in my life. I was filled with true peace, convicted with a sense of purpose.

The more I preached in Pensacola, the more our little group began to realize that God had gathered us together to form a ministry. In 1988, we developed a five-day School of Evangelization program and began presenting it in other parishes.

Invitations soon arrived from other parts of the country and from Canada for us to present our program. We never sought those invitations. The Lord had taught us to walk by faith, relying on him for everything. He provided everything.

The message we presented in the School of Evangelization included what we had learned from our experiences with the Lord and from prayer. The money to support the ministry came from the people who attended the school. Some responded to the grace they received.

When the ministry first began, we didn't realize it would grow beyond just my sharing my testimony at prayer meetings and church services. We were surprised when it did. We were very thankful for the support of Bishop Lorenzo, as well as the wisdom of Father Smith.

After a time, it became clear that God's intention for this ministry was that it be a traveling ministry that called Catholics to respond to the calling of the bishops written at the Second Vatican Council. The bishops had called us to become evangelizers, and we felt that we were supposed to teach Catholics how to do that. We developed a set of tapes explaining our ministry, which Jeanne still mails out to anyone who requests them today.

Before long, I realized I would be spending a lot of time on the road. Or should I say, I would be spending a lot of time in airplanes and at airports. So I decided to study for a pilot's license and ask the Lord for an airplane. It would make traveling much easier.

A few weeks later, I offered a businessman a deal. I wanted to trade my restaurant and office building for twenty-seven acres of land and a small airplane. He agreed, and we exchanged titles to the property.

About three months later, there was a fire in the restaurant, and the building burned to the ground. A portion of the office building was also damaged.

The man was enraged. He had failed to purchase insurance on the buildings, and he lost a great deal. In addition, during the week of the fire, his wife told him she was leaving him. What a mess! He was so angry, that he drove to the airport and stole the airplane he had traded.

I was furious when I found out. *How dare he steal that airplane? Doesn't he know it's a crime? Doesn't he know I need it to do the Lord's work?*

I called him and said, "Either you bring that plane back within one hour, or I'm going to the sheriff's office to file a complaint and have you arrested."

He hung up without a word.

An hour went by, and no airplane. So I got into a car and began driving towards the sheriff's office. While I was on the way, I began praying in tongues. Father Smith had recommended the practice to me.

While I was praying, the Lord spoke to me. "Whose airplane is it?"

"It's yours, Lord."

"Then don't worry about it. I don't want you putting anybody in jail for taking what belongs to me."

I turned the car around and returned to the airport to pick up Jeanne. We drove to my speaking engagement in Alabama. While we were driving, she read the Gospel of Luke to me. She began at chapter one. Nothing seemed significant to me until she got to the sixth chapter, where Jesus said,

> But I tell you who hear me: Love your enemies, do good to those who hate you, bless those who curse you, pray for those who mistreat you. If someone strikes you on one cheek, turn to him the other also. If someone takes your cloak, do not stop him from taking your tunic. Give to everyone who asks you, and if anyone takes what belongs to you, do not demand it back.

Verse 30 leapt out at me: "If anyone takes what is yours, do not demand it back." I knew what I had to do. The Lord did not want me to file charges against the man. He wanted me to let him have the airplane.

I called the man and asked him to forgive me for threatening him. I also told him I would not file charges or threaten him again. He demanded that I return the deed to the twenty-seven acres. My mind returned to the gospel verse, Luke 6:30: "Give to everyone who asks you." I had no choice but to return the land to him, even though I knew I would receive nothing in return, not even my own burned-down restaurant building. So, I signed over the deed and mailed it back to him.

**Luke 6:30: "Give to everyone who asks you."**

Three weeks after my airplane was stolen, I spoke to several prayer groups in Houston, Texas. One evening, a man I didn't know came to a house where a prayer meeting was being held. He had come, not to pray, but to borrow something from the homeowner. He listened to me preach and stayed afterward to talk with me.

I had spoken during the prayer meeting about what I had learned from God's word about not demanding that a robber return something stolen from a Christian.

"Are you serious?" the man asked me. "You're not going to get your airplane back?"

"That's right," I said.

"Well," he said, "I have five airplanes."

"Brother," I said, "I need one of them."

"Let's go to the airport tomorrow, and you can pick one out," he said.

So, we did. Later, he told me that he was overcome with emotion when he saw me fly off with that plane. I had picked the smallest one. But without realizing it, I had chosen his favorite plane. I also found out later that the plane was worth three times as much as the one that had been stolen from me.

I flew that plane back and forth across North America for two years, traveling from parish to parish. After two years, I had it refurbished inside and out. I had a new motor put in it. Then, I returned it to the businessman in Houston.

The next week, I was in Vermont, where another man gave me an even larger plane. I flew that one for eight months. Then, I was on my way to California one day in that airplane from Vermont, and it would only get up to 13,000 feet. And that's just at the top of the mountains. If you've ever flown over the Rocky Mountains at 13,000 feet, dodging the mountain tops, it's the most turbulent, hair-raising, exciting, roller coaster ride you'll ever go on. The old plane was upside down, right side up, left side down, right side over, nose up, and tail down.

I said, "Lord, you got better airplanes than this."

And he said, "You couldn't fly another plane if I gave it to you. You're not qualified."

I flew through passes, getting jerked all over the place. I eventually landed at Fresno, California, on a Sunday morning. I walked into the airport and said, "I want to learn how to fly a twin engine plane."

"When do you want to start?" the guy at the counter said.

"Right now."

"What's the hurry?"

"As soon as I get my license, God's going to give me a twin engine plane."

Isn't that brassy? Some people would say that's presumptuous. No, that's faith. That's believing in God. I wasn't smart enough to have any doubt about what I was believing. If what I heard when I was flying through those mountains was true, God had promised to give me a plane.

■ α ■
**I wasn't smart enough to have any doubt about what I was believing.**
■ Ω ■

I went up on a Monday morning and told the instructor I wouldn't fly with him unless he prayed with me. I took his hand, and I said "God, I want you to take this man's mind and give me his knowledge and his wisdom. Let me learn how to fly this airplane as good as he can so that I can get my ticket to fly. And I thank you Jesus."

We got up in the air, and I started pulling knobs and levers, just like the instructor did.

He said, "You're pulling my leg. You already know how to fly."

After the first lesson, we landed the plane. There was a note stuck on his telephone for me to call a man in San Jose, California.

I called, and the man said, "When are you coming over to see us in San Jose?"

I said, "I don't know. I'm taking flying lessons."

"Why?"

I said, "Because when I get my license, God's going to give me a twin engine plane."

There was silence on the line for a minute. I had only met this guy once, and I wasn't sure what he was thinking.

Finally, he said, "I'll tell you what. You get that license, and I'll buy you a plane."

I turned to that fellow at the airport and said, "I want to buy an airplane."

He said, "What kind?"

I said, "I don't know." I didn't know anything about twin engine planes. "I want something that will fly high and fly fast. I want something that will get me over the mountains without bouncing me to death. I'm getting too old to be bounced like that."

He said, "You want a pressurized Aerostar. It flies 300 miles an hour."

I said, "I'll take it."

He said, "You're serious, aren't you?"

I said, "Get me a plane."

Jeanne came out, and in nine days, I passed my test and had my license. On the fifth day, that man had purchased me a slick tan and white airplane with an orange and brown stripe. It cost $160,000, and he paid cash for it. I gave them that little old single engine plane, and I got the instructor to take me around and show me how to take off and land the new Aerostar.

When I landed it in Pensacola two weeks later, the people at the airport asked, "Where did you get the plane?"

I told them.

"Show us your license."

You know what they accused me of? Hypnotism. They did.

They said, "What do you do, hypnotize people? How'd you get that plane?"

"Jesus gave it to me," I said.

Our ministry became a faith ministry. We had no budgets or fund-raising efforts, no plans or programs. We accepted invitations to preach whenever we could, and we relied on the Lord to give us whatever we needed to minister. We discovered that the more faith we put in God, the more he blessed us.

> ■ α ■
> **The more faith we put in God, the more he blessed us.**
> ■ Ω ■

**The Parable of the Persistent Widow**

¹Then Jesus told his disciples a parable to show them that they should always pray and not give up. ²He said: "In a certain town there was a judge who neither feared God nor cared what people thought. ³And there was a widow in that town who kept coming to him with the plea, 'Grant me justice against my adversary.'

⁴"For some time he refused. But finally he said to himself, 'Even though I don't fear God or care what people think, ⁵yet because this widow keeps bothering me, I will see that she gets justice, so that she won't eventually come and attack me!'"

⁶ And the Lord said, "Listen to what the unjust judge says. ⁷And will not God bring about justice for his chosen ones, who cry out to him day and night? Will he keep putting them off? ⁸I tell you, he will see that they get justice, and quickly. However, when the Son of Man comes, will he find faith on the earth?"

**Luke 18:1–8**

**The Parable of the Pharisee and the Tax Collector**
⁹To some who were confident of their own righteousness and looked down on everyone else, Jesus told this parable: ¹⁰"Two men went up to the temple to pray, one a Pharisee and the other a tax collector. ¹¹The Pharisee stood by himself and prayed: 'God, I thank you that I am not like other people—robbers, evildoers, adulterers—or even like this tax collector. ¹²I fast twice a week and give a tenth of all I get.'

¹³"But the tax collector stood at a distance. He would not even look up to heaven, but beat his breast and said, 'God, have mercy on me, a sinner.'

¹⁴"I tell you that this man, rather than the other, went home justified before God. For all those who exalt themselves will be humbled, and those who humble themselves will be exalted."

**Luke 18:9–14**

CHAPTER EIGHT

# On the Road for Jesus

## Charlie Desires a Television Ministry

When my preaching ministry first began to develop, I didn't fully understand the gift that God had given me. I just knew that the Holy Spirit had given me wisdom which he wanted me to place at the service of the church.

This wisdom concerned the authority and tradition of the Catholic Church and how Scripture can be understood in the light of that authority and tradition. As I began to understand Scripture more fully, I proclaimed these truths as a layman. The people I talked to understood what I was saying, and some suggested that I preach on television.

For four years, I strongly desired to tell the millions who watch Christian television about unconditional love and lay people ministering in faith. But it was only a desire. I had no idea how to make that desire a reality. However, I believe that God wanted to make it a reality. And since I knew that God can do anything, I didn't worry about it or even look for someone to put me on the air.

The Lord taught me to look at desires and hopes with eyes of faith. I placed the whole idea of television into God's hands. That doesn't mean I didn't speak about it to people. I surely did. But I didn't worry. I knew that God had a plan. I just needed to patiently walk in faith until he made his plan known to me.

God began to reveal the first phase of his plan in January of 1983. I was preaching that

> ■ α ■
> **I placed the whole idea of television into God's hands.**
> ■ Ω ■

month in Calexico, California. One day, a renowned Pentecostal leader called to tell me that a friend of his from Denver, Colorado, had asked him to recommend a Catholic evangelist who could minister to his people. This friend from Denver was the pastor of a large Pentecostal congregation which counted among its members hundreds of former Catholics.

When I arrived at the church in Denver, I noticed that it was full of television equipment for the church's own productions. I told the pastor about our week-long School of Evangelization that I had been conducting in Catholic churches. I said, "Would you be interested in holding one in your church and taping it for possible television broadcast?"

"That's a great idea," the pastor said. "It would teach our congregation how our Catholic brothers and sisters win souls for Jesus. Let's do it!"

"Okay," I said. "Now all we need is the permission of your bishop."

"I don't have a bishop," he said. "This is a non-denominational church."

"Yes, you do," I said. "He's down the street at the Catholic Pastoral Center. His name is Archbishop Grant. Why don't you go down and ask him if I can come into your church and present my seminar on Catholic evangelism?"

The pastor did that, and Archbishop Grant gave us permission. We decided to conduct the school during February of 1984. We agreed to tape all the sessions. Because I suspected that this was going to be the beginning of my television ministry, I left Denver, rejoicing in the new plan that the Lord was revealing.

One year later, I was in southern California, preparing for the seminar in Denver. I had prayed all year for this new television ministry. The pastor in Denver had agreed to videotape the seminar, and when the teaching was over, he planned to hand me the seminar tapes. I would have to figure out what to do with them from that point.

Shortly before leaving for Denver, Jeanne and I were at a restaurant in San Diego with another couple. We were talking enthusiastically about the wonderful things the Lord was doing in our ministry. We were especially happy about the additional means we saw in television for us to bring his message to the whole world.

While we were talking, a young man approached us and said, "My name is Bruce Cooley. It is really exciting to hear someone talk about Jesus."

"Yes," I said. "Everyone at this table is really excited about Jesus."

Bruce gave me his business card and told me to contact him if I ever needed his services. Then he left, without saying what those services were. Since I was in the middle of lunch, I put the card in my pocket without reading it. A few minutes later, I was told I was wanted on the telephone.

When I picked up the phone, the voice on the other end said, "This is Bruce Cooley. I came to your table a little while ago and left you my card. But I really didn't do what I was supposed to do. I was supposed to offer you my services. Is there anything I can do to help you?"

"Brother," I said, "what do you do?"

"I'm an audio-video technician. I put together television programs for businesses."

So, I told him about the plans we had for videotaping in Denver. "I really need someone to take charge of that material once it's on tape."

"I'd like to do that for you," Bruce said.

We met together and decided that God was calling Bruce to be part of Good News Ministries. The ministry purchased a commercial-grade television camera and a portable videotape pack. Bruce then followed us around, taking shots of everything we did. He would later edit the videos and use them to create introductory and closing segments for our program.

The Denver taping did not go well at all, and we have never used the tapes. But we now had Bruce and all his expertise. Soon, we purchased additional television equipment in order to do our own taping.

> **God was calling Bruce to be part of Good News Ministries.**

One evening, while I was conducting a School of Evangelization in Alberta, Canada, I mentioned that we hoped someday to televise the school. "The only obstacle to this dream becoming a reality," I said, "is the cost."

The next evening, a woman came up to me after my presentation and handed me a cashier's check for $27,000, to be used for the television ministry. We used that money to purchase video recorders and other equipment. At this point, we had about half of what was needed to produce quality programs.

Three weeks later, I was at the Pensacola airport when a man charged up and said, "Is that your airplane?" The plane had a big dove painted on the tail, along with the words, 'Jesus is Lord,' over the windows. We had also painted 'Good News Ministries' and the words 'Holy Ghost Airlines' on the sides.

"Yes," I said.

"What church do you belong to?"

"The Catholic Church," I said.

He stared at me and said, "So do I, but I've never heard of anything like this."

"Well," I said, "Get used to it, because this is the future of the church. Catholics are discovering what it means to give their lives to Jesus. It's only a matter of time before Catholics by the millions will begin reaching out to the whole world with the excitement of the Holy Spirit."

The man told me about his two daughters who had recently left the Catholic Church to join a church whose Pentecostal leader preached against Catholicism. This man's family was in the middle of a serious spiritual crisis.

I didn't have time to talk with him, because I was scheduled to fly out of Pensacola just a few minutes later. I gave him a set of evangelization tapes.

> "No one has ever explained the faith to me like this."

"Listen to these," I said, "and then give them to your daughters. I believe it will help you solve your problem."

Later, he called me. "I listened to the entire set of tapes in the last twenty-four hours. I've never heard anything like this before," he said. "I've been a Catholic all my life, studied for years under Jesuits, and attended all kinds of retreats and seminars. But no one has ever explained the faith to me like this. I have really been blessed."

In one of those tapes, I had mentioned that we needed $16,000 for additional television equipment. This man was so moved by what he had heard on the tapes that he wanted to help our ministry.

"Where can I send a check?" he asked.

A few days later, his check for $16,000 arrived in the mail. We used it to purchase the additional equipment we needed.

The following week, we gave the evangelization seminar in Phoenix, Arizona, where the Lord deeply touched several people who contributed a total of $21,000.

All during this time, Bruce Cooley traveled with me, taping most of my talks. One day, he told me that we finally had enough equipment and enough raw tape to begin a television program. So, I asked him to call someone in the Christian television business to find out how much a weekly program would cost. We had already spent more than $80,000 on equipment and taping, and we still hadn't put a single minute of our message on the air.

Bruce called Trinity Broadcasting, a Christian network based in the Los Angeles area. He told a sales representative that we were interested in buying time.

"Who are you?" she asked.

Bruce told her that we were a Catholic evangelistic organization.

"A Catholic evangelist! I've never heard of a Catholic evangelist!"

This woman, who had grown up a Catholic, but had joined another church, became intrigued with our ministry and decided to come to Arizona to hear me preach. She brought another Trinity staff member with her, and they stayed for two days, listening to our teaching and talking to us. When they left, they seemed excited about what we were doing. They tentatively offered us a $3,300 per hour time slot.

The thought of spending $3,300 a week for television time, plus the additional cost of equipment, personnel, and so on would frighten most people. That's a great deal of money. But this ministry is a faith ministry. I didn't waste a single moment worrying, because I knew the Lord was leading the way. If God wanted a weekly television program featuring a Catholic lay evangelist, he would supply the money we needed.

So, I said, "Lord, you've given us all this equipment. So please provide the rest of what we need."

And God did. We received a donation in the amount we needed within a few days.

> **If God wanted a weekly television program featuring a Catholic lay evangelist, he would supply the money we needed.**

Two weeks later, I was preaching in Mammoth, a small mining town in the mountains of Arizona, when Paul Crouch, the president of Trinity Broadcasting Network, called and asked me to meet with him in California in December of 1984.

I arranged to have at that meeting three men who had been supporting our ministry: a past president of the Ramada Inn motel chain, the man from Louisiana who had given us the $16,000, and an airline captain. Each of them had encountered the Lord through our ministry, and each one was also an astute businessman. I wanted them to advise me at the meeting with Paul Crouch.

Paul Crouch proposed a contract that did not include the $3,300 charge. Instead, the network wanted to sponsor me, and they even offered us the use of their studios. Paul explained all the details, proposing a thirty-minute prime-time slot.

The airline captain listened to this, then spoke up. "Charlie can't even say his name in thirty minutes," he said. "He needs at least an hour."

The program director, who was responsible for scheduling, said, "We don't have an hour available. All we have is thirty minutes."

"We may not have an hour," Paul said, "but we'll find one. We want your program, and you'll have that hour."

During our meeting, Paul Crouch said he was very impressed with the Second Vatican Council's Decree on the Apostolate of Lay People. The network representatives who had attended the seminar had taken several copies of the decree back with them, and Paul had read it. He said, "My own Assemblies of God church should adopt this document as a guideline for lay ministry."

He was excited about the document, about the spiritual vitality he saw coming from the Catholic community, and about my God-given ability to preach. Paul was also impressed with Catholicism for personal reasons. His eldest son had been baptized in the Holy Spirit in the Catholic Church. Several people in his organization also had close ties with the Catholic Church.

While we were in California discussing our program, Paul asked Jeanne and me to appear as guests on his show, *Praise the Lord*. Our appearance generated a great response from viewers. The greatest excitement was over my being a Catholic. The Protestant viewers just loved to hear a Catholic lay evangelist preach to them about Jesus.

**The Protestant viewers just loved to hear a Catholic lay evangelist preach to them about Jesus.**

We expected God to provide great things through this television ministry. We had been given enough money to purchase almost all the equipment we needed, and now we had received free time on a nationwide network. However, God had something more in mind.

Not long after our meetings with Trinity, I conducted an evangelization seminar at a parish in the San Diego area. One morning, I walked out of the home where I was staying, and I saw a bus parked there. I wouldn't have given that bus a second thought, except that it was painted in the same colors as my airplane. It was white on top, tan on the bottom, and it had an orange and brown stripe running around it.

I turned to my host and said, "Sam, your bus is painted the same colors as my airplane. I wonder if the Lord is telling me something about that bus."

"Well," he said, "I hope not, because I plan to convert it into a motor home so my wife and I can travel around the country."

I couldn't stop looking at that bus. Something was stirring inside me.

"Where did you get that bus?" I asked.

Sam said, "I bought it from a dealer here in San Diego. He's got a whole fleet of nineteen-foot Mercedes diesel buses that he bought from a mass transit company. He's selling them, one at a time."

*I can't do anything about buying one of those buses yet.*

For an entire month, that bus was never far from my mind. Then one day, I felt that God wanted me to buy one of those buses. A man in the parish where I was speaking gave our ministry $7,300, so I went to the dealer's lot and bought a bus.

> **I felt that God wanted me to buy one of those buses.**

The dealer serviced the bus and told us it was ready to go. We headed east, but the bus didn't make it over the mountain. We had to have it towed back to San Diego. I called the dealer and asked him to service it again. If it couldn't make if over that mountain, it would be of no use to us.

I left Bruce to look after the bus, and I flew to Yuma, Arizona, to present another School of Evangelization. Meanwhile, the dealer in California got the bus running again, and Bruce drove it over the mountain and through the desert to Yuma. But when he got to Yuma, the engine blew up.

That seemed like the last straw. The bus would never run the way we needed it to.

I said, "Bruce, sell the bus to a junkyard."

That night, while I was preaching in Yuma, I told the story about the bus.

Afterwards, a man came forward and said, "I can rebuild the engine of your bus for you."

"Praise the Lord!" I said.

He and his associates set to work. They rebuilt the engine, the fuel system, and the cooling system—all the running parts. When they were finished, that little bus ran great.

While they were finishing their work, a man named Chuck called to say that he had heard me preach on television, had ordered my tapes, and had experienced the Lord very powerfully through them. He had been separated from his wife, but after hearing our teaching, he had been reconciled with her. He was so excited.

"The Lord impressed upon me that you needed a generator," he said. "I've got a 5,000 watt electric model. Can you use it?"

I said, "I've got a bus that's being repaired in Yuma. We are turning it into a television studio so that we can produce television programs while we travel."

"Great!" he said. "Does it need to be painted?"

"It's in bad shape," I said. "It's all banged up and really could use a paint job."

"Well, I own a paint and body shop," he said, "and I'd love to straighten it up for you."

Chuck and his crew did a fine job on that bus. They took out most of the windows and replaced them with metal panels so that we could do television work inside. Then, they flushed the bus out, repaired all the dents in the exterior, and painted it. When they were finished, it looked magnificent, and it made a great studio.

**That bus made a great studio.**

Meanwhile, I contacted a couple in Fort Worth, Texas, who had offered to do cabinet work for me. Chuck drove the bus to Fort Worth, and the couple in Fort Worth built cabinets for all the television equipment.

In less than six months, the Lord took us from one television camera with a twenty-minute portable tape pack to ownership of more than $100,000 worth of equipment mounted in beautiful cabinets in a completely rebuilt Mercedes-Benz bus.

Our maiden voyage in the bus was to Toledo, Ohio. When we arrived there, a man approached me after our session one night and said, "I was just out looking at your bus, and I noticed that it needs new tires. I own a tire store. Would you let me put a new set on for you?"

We televised our Christian program, *On the Road for Jesus*, for eight years. A man from Yuma, Arizona paid for all of our air time. Our goal was never to make money from our shows. Any money that we did make was donated to *Praise the Lord* on Trinity Broadcasting Network. We were very blessed to have Bruce Cooley's gifts in directing our show until it went off the air. He moved on to work as a radio announcer in San Diego.

When our television ministry was over, we no longer needed our beautiful Mercedes-Benz bus with all of its television equipment. But God wasn't finished with it yet. We donated it to some people from Yuma, Arizona. They removed all of the equipment from it and filled it up with food for hungry people in Mexico. Each week, they drove it across the border from Yuma to bless the people who needed to feel the love of Jesus in a real way.

When we first bought the bus for our television ministry, it was a wreck. By the time God was finished with it, our bus was one of the most attractive ones on the road, with a sign painted on the back that read, 'On the Road for Jesus.' I was once a wreck, too, but through the mercy and the grace of God, I had been transformed into a beautiful vehicle of his love. I was ready to go anywhere on the road for Jesus.

> **We televised our Christian program, *On the Road for Jesus*, for eight years.**

### The Believers Share Their Possessions

³²All the believers were one in heart and mind. No one claimed that any of his possessions was his own, but they shared everything they had. ³³With great power the apostles continued to testify to the resurrection of the Lord Jesus, and much grace was upon them all. ³⁴There were no needy persons among them. For from time to time those who owned lands or houses sold them, brought the money from the sales ³⁵and put it at the apostles' feet, and it was distributed to anyone as he had need.

³⁶Joseph, a Levite from Cyprus, whom the apostles called Barnabas (which means Son of Encouragement), ³⁷sold a field he owned and brought the money and put it at the apostles' feet.

**Acts 4:32–37**

Life can be very confusing. Without God's direction, we often do not know which way to go. Charlie tried to figure out which way to head when he encountered this sign in Africa.

Charlie visited Nakuru, Kenya, where he preached while a young priest translated his message.

Charlie explained the Decree on the Apostolate of Lay People at the Good News School of Evangelization.

Charlie with his student. Students travel from many countries to attend the Good News School of Evangelization. Francis Muroki flew from Kenya to learn all that he could about Jesus, then returned to his village to encourage others to do the same.

Charlie and Jeanne feel blessed to be at home in Pensacola once again, where the Good News School of Evangelization is sponsored by St. Anne's Catholic Church.

Today, Charlie serves as the Director for the Good News School of Evangelization.

Charlie and Mother Teresa ministered to people in Tijuana who were physically and spiritually dying.

CHAPTER NINE

# Learning to Love as Jesus Does

## Charlie Learns What it Takes to Love

I was ready to go anywhere for Jesus, and I remembered something that I had learned from Father Smith years earlier. After I had committed my life to Jesus, Father Smith began to teach me about forgiveness and unconditional love. He showed me the Scriptures that commanded me to love everyone—people who had hurt me, as well as those who had been good to me.

"You mean I have to love the man who molested my children?" I had asked in disbelief. "It's hard enough to think about forgiving him. The idea of loving him makes me ill."

Father Smith was a good and gentle man, but he kept confronting me with the truth. He showed me Jesus' words in Matthew 6:14–15:

> For if you forgive men when they sin against you, your heavenly Father will also forgive you. But if you do not forgive men their sins, your Father will not forgive your sins.

He also pointed out God's truth about unconditional love in Luke 6:27, 35:

> But I tell you who hear me: Love your enemies, do good to those who hate you . . . and lend to them without expecting to get anything back. Then your reward will be great, and you will be sons of the Most High, because he is kind to the ungrateful and wicked.

As I prayed about those Scriptures and recalled how much the Lord had forgiven me, I realized that I had no choice but to forgive *everyone* who had offended me. I had already forgiven Jeanne. That was relatively easy, because when I experienced the love of the Lord Jesus in my life, I came to love her. But it was not so easy with everyone.

> **I realized that if God had ever stopped loving me during my years of sin, I would have died and gone to hell.**

When I accepted that I must forgive *all* who offended me and love them because God loves them, I realized that if God had ever stopped loving me during my years of sin, I would have died and gone to hell. If Jeanne had held grievances against me, it would have been difficult for me to surrender my life to Jesus. When she forgave me, she released me from the many sins I'd committed against her. Jesus tells us in Matthew 18:18:

> I tell you the truth, whatever you bind on earth will be bound in heaven, and whatever you loose on earth will be loosed in heaven.

Many Catholics think that this passage refers only to the authority of the clergy to forgive sins in Jesus' name in the sacrament of reconciliation. But the authority of the clergy is actually based more on another passage, Matthew 16:19, where Jesus confers the power to bind and loose on Peter and his successors—the bishops and priests of the church.

When God tells us to be merciful and to love unconditionally, he means that we are to love *everyone*. Whether they are attractive or unattractive, good or wicked, we must love them, because our Father in heaven loves them. Jesus commands us to be perfect, just as our heavenly Father is perfect. Matthew 5:48 reads, "Be perfect, therefore, as your heavenly Father is perfect."

Most people today, even Christians, do not understand what love is. Many of us have never seriously considered what the Scriptures say about love. For example, I John 4:8 reads, "Whoever does not love does not love God, because God is love." In I John 4:10–12, 20–21, we can learn even more about love:

> This is love: not that we loved God, but that he loved us and sent his Son as an atoning sacrifice for our sins. Dear friends, since God so loved us, we also ought to love one another. No one has ever seen God; but if we love one another, God lives in us and his love

is made complete in us. If anyone says, "I love God," yet hates his brother, he is a liar. For anyone who does not love his brother, whom he has seen, cannot love God, whom he has not seen. And he has given us this command: Whoever loves God must also love his brother.

In these verses, John says that if you don't love the brother you can see, you don't love the God you cannot see. If you don't love your brother, he says, but say you love God, you're a liar.

We must love unconditionally, as does the Lord. Matthew 5:44-45 reads,

> ■ α ■
> **If you don't love your brother, but say you love God, you're a liar.**
> ■ Ω ■

> But I tell you: Love your enemies and pray for those who persecute you, that you may be sons of your Father in heaven. He causes his sun to rise on the evil and the good, and sends rain on the righteous and the unrighteous.

When I learned to forgive my neighbor *and* love him unconditionally, it reaped everlasting rewards. I'm convinced that my neighbor and I will meet again in heaven.

The message of love is at the heart of our Christian faith. We love others, because God first loved us, and to be true to his love, we must love everyone. Some Christians interpret the Scripture passages about love as referring only to loving other Christians. After all, John uses the word, 'brother.' Who is our brother? The Nicene Creed says, "I believe in one God, the Father, the Almighty, maker of heaven and earth, of all that is seen and unseen."

If God is the Maker of all, then all human beings belong to him. We may wonder, *even those who have not accepted his love?* Yes. Scripture clearly shows that God loves all his creatures. This is our call, also.

When a lawyer confronted Jesus with the question, "Who is my neighbor?" Jesus told him the parable of the Good Samaritan in Luke 10:25-35. In verses 36-37, Jesus answered the man's question with a question:

> "Which of these three do you think was a neighbor to the man who fell into the hands of robbers?" The expert in the law replied, "The one who had mercy on him." Jesus told him, "Go and do likewise."

This passage also teaches us what love is. Love is caring for another. Love is having compassion for another. Love is serving the needs of another. In his famous teaching on using the gifts of the Holy Spirit in love, the Apostle Paul tells us in I Corinthians 13:4–7, 13:

> Love is patient, love is kind. It does not envy, it does not boast, it is not self-seeking, it is not easily angered, it keeps no record of wrongs. Love does not delight in evil but rejoices with the truth. It always protects, always trusts, always hopes, always perseveres. Love never fails. And now these three remain: faith, hope and love. But the greatest of these is love.

Christians are to love. It is our first and highest calling. Everything we do should flow from the love of God which fills our hearts. If we do not love, we are not doing God's work.

> **If we do not love, we are not doing God's work.**

Learning about love from the teachings of Scripture and the church set me free internally. My relationships with my children—which had been very poor because of my years of drinking and chasing the dollar—were gradually healed. I learned to share the love of God; not only with them, but with everyone I met. I learned that the only way to evangelize is to love people into the kingdom of God.

When, by the grace of God, I decided to love the neighbor who had molested my children, I was able to evangelize him. I didn't preach at him or berate him for his sin. I forgave him. I loved him. The result was repentance. That's real evangelism. That's loving people into the kingdom of God.

When I realized the power of love, I knew that I could also love my children into the kingdom of God. They had all rejected God and the church, primarily because of my bad example. They had seen me go to church, yet fail to live the faith. So, they tuned church out. They rebelled against authority, which they had also learned from me.

I needed to live what I preached in order to undo the effects of many years of bad example. I had to be patient, control my anger, and put the concerns of others ahead of my own. For me, it meant learning a completely new way of relating. It took years. I had to put off the mind of Charlie Osburn and put on the mind of Christ. The mind of Christ is love—self-sacrificing love—for others. Philippians 2:5–8 tells us:

Your attitude should be the same as that of Christ Jesus: who, being in very nature God, did not consider equality with God something to be grasped, but made himself nothing, taking the very nature of a servant, being made in human likeness. And being found in appearance as a man, he humbled himself and became obedient to death—even death on a cross!

Jesus' love covers a multitude of sins. If he could cover mine, I had to come to the realization that he could cover my children's, too. It was time for me to stop judging them, condemning them, and heaping guilt on them. I made up my mind to love them unconditionally for the rest of my life, no matter what they did. I only have the power to forgive, not judge. Jesus is our only judge.

> ■ α ■
> **It was time for me to stop judging them, condemning them, and heaping guilt on them.**
> ■ Ω ■

Some people accused me of being an enabler. They asked me if I was planning to raise a bunch of delinquents. I thought about it, and I came to the conclusion that God is the greatest enabler of all time. Through the blood of Christ, he forgives us for everything. We can't change people by criticizing and brow-beating them. All we can do is love them. God will change their hearts.

One day, the sheriff's department called me. At the time, I was the mayor of Warrington, and they called me at my office. Craig was in jail, because he had been caught drag racing on a city street. He had never been in trouble with the law before, and I could have let him sit in jail for a while to 'learn his lesson.' But I don't think that would have displayed the unconditional love which God calls us to show.

So, I dropped what I was doing and drove over to the jail. When I was taken to the entrance of the jail, I shouted from the doorway, "Where is the son of the most high God?"

Craig was crying when I got to his cell.

I said, "Son, don't you know that I love you?" I was concerned that he had perceived a lack of love in me and was getting into trouble in order to strike back.

"Yes, Daddy," he said, "I know you love me."

"Let's go home, then."

When we got outside, Craig said, "I'm sorry, Daddy, I won't ever do that again."

I said, "Whether you spend your entire life in jail or become a productive citizen, I won't love you any differently. You have to choose what you're going to do with your life."

I decided to love my son—to stand by him—no matter what he had done. Jeanne and I had to stand by him and patiently pray for him for six troubled years. During those years, he became increasingly rebellious. I could have tried to change him. I could have preached at him, yelled at him, or thrown him out of the house. Many people would have advocated doing these things, calling it 'tough love.' I decided not to. I wanted to follow what the gospel teaches about love.

> "You have to choose what you're going to do with your life."

During those six years of patiently loving our son and praying for him, Jeanne and I were challenged many times. He was a rebellious young man, and he was hurting. We rarely saw him. We knew that only when his heart was filled with the love of Jesus, would he be healed of those hurts. We longed with all our hearts for him to commit his life to the Lord, but we knew that he had to decide that for himself.

No one can force a decision for Jesus Christ on someone else. All we could do was continually show him the love of Jesus, doing our best to love him into the kingdom of God.

One night, Craig was sitting on a barstool having some drinks with a friend.

His friend said, "If I had a gun right now, I would blow my brains out, I'm so bored."

Craig heard a voice saying, "If he kills himself, you will be held responsible, because you know what you are supposed to be telling him."

That night, Craig showed up at the side of our bed. He knelt down and said, "I've had enough of the life I've been living, and I want to invite Jesus into my heart."

A few weeks later, on Father's Day, the five Osburn children gave me a new Bible, each one writing a message in it. Craig had written: "I love you, Dad, for loving me into the kingdom of God."

After we first started televising our program, I had to fly from San Francisco to Pensacola. By the time I got home, I was exhausted. While I was sleeping that night, I dreamed that I was in a house full of tables of beautiful food. Every room I entered was full of food, and I went from table to table, eating.

Suddenly, two men came up, handcuffed me, and took me to a car, without a word. They drove to an abandoned field with a high iron fence. I knew it was a jail. When I asked why I was being jailed, the two men refused to answer. They just got back into the car and drove away.

Well, this imprisonment agitated me, and I asked the Lord, "What's going on here?"

"You're in jail."

"I can see that, Lord. What I want to know is why."

No answer.

"Well then, what do I have to do to get out?"

"Fast and pray."

"For how long?"

"Fourteen days."

"Fourteen days! I can't go fourteen days without food."

"Then stay in jail."

I woke up in a sweat and told Jeanne about the dream. "I have to fast for fourteen days—no food at all. Nothing but water."

Jeanne supported me, of course. I couldn't have made it without her.

On the fourth day of the fast, I went to our office to work. I was feeling very weak by then, and when I got there, all I could do was lie down on the sofa. My son, Brian, was in the office. He wore his hair long and had a beard and strange-looking clothes. He'd been working with us for about two years, but he had not committed his life to the Lord. Nevertheless, I treated him exactly the way I preach. I was patient, kind, and loving with him. For eight years, I had been loving my son into the kingdom of God.

I quickly finished the business I had gone to the office to do, and then I left.

After I was gone, Brian looked over at his mother and said, "Mom, what's wrong with Dad?"

"I'm really supposed to keep this quiet," she said, "But I can tell you, Brian. Your father is on a fourteen-day fast."

"Dad can't fast for fourteen days."

"I know that, you know that, and Dad knows that. But God apparently knows something different, because he ordered it."

That conversation really affected Brian. I wasn't there, of course, but Jeanne told me that a few minutes after her conversation with him, Brian got up out of his chair without saying a word. An hour later, he came back clean shaven and with his hair cut short.

"I've just committed my life to Jesus," he said, "I'm giving you notice that I'm here to serve the Lord Jesus Christ."

That was the first miracle of the fast. The second miracle occurred on the ninth day. I was in the office when an editor from *New Covenant* magazine called. *New Covenant* is a magazine devoted to spiritual renewal in the Catholic Church. The editor told Brian that they wanted to feature an article about me and to put my picture on the cover.

After that article was published in September 1983, we received telephone calls and letters from all over the world. And that was the month our television ministry began to move from dream to reality.

I still don't fully understand why God wanted me to fast those fourteen days, but I know the fruit of it. My son committed his life to Jesus and was released from his own kind of prison. And our ministry began to take on international significance.

I was overwhelmed at the goodness of God. He never allows loving actions to go unrewarded. The Bible is full of promises for those who trust in God and obey him. What better reward is there for Christian parents than to see their children give their lives to Jesus?

Each one of our children had gone through tremendously traumatic experiences earlier in their lives. I believe those experiences were meant to teach me how to love others whom I would meet later in life.

My daughter, Amy, came to me several years ago and said, "Dad, I found the guy that I want to marry, but he's a mess." She went on. "I really like him, but he doesn't have any of your qualities. None. Would you let the two of us live with you so you can help me love him? I can't love him by myself. I'm going to need help."

When we begin our conversion as Christians, we usually work with people who are down and out—like alcoholics, drug addicts, people who are out of control, and homosexuals. Our kids grew up with that, so when Amy grew up and met this guy that was a really big mess, she had an attraction to him. Jesus was always attracted to the suffering of other people.

So, Amy said "Dad, I want to marry this guy, and I'm going to need you to help me love him. I don't think I can do it by myself, so can we live in your house?" I knew when she asked, that I was going to get checked out to see how much I love. Other people will check you out when you start this walk. So Amy moved

> Other people will check you out, when you start this walk.

in along with her husband, David. They had their first baby, then they had their second baby.

David really couldn't talk to me at first. Here's the way we communicated. He would steal things from the house and take them to the pawn shop and hock them. Then I'd go to the pawn shop and bring them home so he could steal them again. That's the way we communicated. He knew that I knew he was stealing.

So, when David finally realized that I knew what he was doing, he went out and wrote $6,000 worth of bad checks.

I said "Boy, this is really going to be a test for me."

The police came and arrested David. They put him in jail, and I went right down and bailed him out.

I said "David, you know we've got to cover these checks. I'm going to do all I can to help you."

So I just started calling people and saying, "I've got one of the members of my family who's really in trouble. Could you send me some money?"

People would send me $100, or $200, or maybe $500, all depending on who they were. I raised $6,000 in two days. I made David go with me, and we went around and picked up every bad check. And while I was there, I asked the people to forgive my family and to forgive David for what we had done.

The problem with David was that I didn't know how to communicate with him, and I didn't understand his needs. Everybody has needs. Some people know how to ask for them, and some people don't. Some people don't have enough resources to take care of their needs themselves. David was the most pitiful guy I've ever met in my whole life. And I know how desperately I needed him to teach me. I'm a slow learner.

People gave their lives to Jesus while we were picking up those checks. God can use all things for good. All things work together for good if you don't have a hard heart. David has taught me more than anybody on this earth how to love. And he's still teaching me.

> ■ α ■
> **God can use all things for good.**
> ■ Ω ■

Covering all of those bad checks didn't change David one bit at the time. But I changed. I can never expect anybody to change. I can't bring change to anybody but myself. So my approach to all situations is that I know it's going to help me.

One morning while David and Amy were living with us, I came out of my room to catch a six o'clock flight, so it was really early.

David was standing outside, waiting for me. He was a child. He was 6'4" and weighed 250 pounds. He said "Peepa, I'm your problem around here—"

I interrupted him and said, "David, you are not my problem."

And he said, "But I don't want to be like this no more."

I said "David, I like you just the way you are. You don't have to change for me. If you want to change, you change for yourself."

> **God sends really special people for me to learn from.**

There have been changes—tremendous changes. But life can only teach me. It doesn't teach anybody else for me. I learn from everyone that I come into contact with. God sends really special people for me to learn from.

## Jeanne Remembers How David Changed Her Heart

David lived in our house for ten years. While he was there, I began to serve him, too. There were fourteen people living in our household. We had a three-bedroom, two-bath ranch. Where the double carport was, we built on another bedroom and bath. David, Amy, and their children stayed back there. They were contained in one room off the kitchen. I would often find their clothes sitting in the washer or the dryer. I had a choice to make. I had to either fold those clothes like they were Charlie's and mine with a lot of love and care, or throw them on the floor. Or I could throw the wet ones up on top of the dryer and leave the dry ones in the dryer just to let them get wrinkled. I made the decision that every time I went into the laundry room, I was going to fold up their clothes with a lot of love.

Some nights, I got home late. It was one o'clock in the morning when I went to bed. Believe it or not, out of the fourteen people who stayed in our house, David was the only one that would go in and help me in the kitchen late at night.

There'd be some nights when he'd say "Meema, the kitchen's mine. I'll take care of everything."

Or there would be times when I would come home, and the kitchen would be perfectly clean. Some years later, he began cooking. He does that now, with his family. He stays home and takes care of the children. He cooks for them, he washes, and he does chores. He didn't know how to do those things until he came to live with us.

## Charlie Never Gives Up on His Kids

Several years ago, our daughter, Regina, was in bad shape. She had been in a state of depression for twelve years, to the point where the doctor said there was no hope. She had gone over the edge . . . she was a vegetable. She weighed 400 pounds. From the time she was about twenty-three or twenty-four, she had started living a life of drugs and alcohol. She just slept all day and ate all night.

When Jeanne and I got a telephone call one afternoon, we learned that Regina's husband had beaten her up and broken her arm. The kids thought she was going to die. So we rushed her to the hospital, and they had her lying up on the table, bleeding. The doctor was examining her, and he discovered that her husband had burned her stomach with cigarettes. He had sat on her and just fried her meat.

The doctor said, "This woman's been tortured—call the police."

So the police came, and they started asking me questions.

And I answered all the questions.

Then a policeman asked me to sign the piece of paper that he'd been writing on.

I asked him, "What am I signing?"

He said, "This is an arrest warrant."

"Oh," I said, "We're not going to arrest him. We've already forgiven him."

> ■ α ■
> "This woman's been tortured—call the police."
> ■ Ω ■

The policeman went out and told the doctor that we weren't going to have Regina's husband arrested. Well, the doctor went berserk! And, if there wouldn't have been a male nurse and a female nurse that jumped in between the doctor and Jeanne and I, we would have been physically attacked by that doctor.

The doctor was screaming at me, "You yellow-bellied coward, you pinko! People like you need to be in an insane asylum! Your whole family's a bunch of [expletive deleted]."

Vulgar language was just pouring out at Jeanne and me. This male nurse had Jeanne and me held tight together, and another nurse was there holding back the doctor. That male nurse whispered in my ear, "You're the first Christian that I've ever met."

So the doctor ordered us to take Regina out of the hospital—just the way she was. "Get her out of here! Right now, get her out of my hospital! Get her out of here now!"

I had to go out and get the ambulance people to come in and take her and put her back in the ambulance. She had to come to my house and stay, because her husband had already moved in with another woman.

Jeanne and I just walked the floor that night and prayed, "Lord, she belongs to you. She's not really ours. You've given her to us to love and to serve, and if it's time for her to go home, we release her to you. She's yours." And then we went to bed.

When I woke up the next morning, I smelled coffee. I got up and went to the kitchen, and there stood Regina, making coffee.

I said "Regina, how do you feel?"

She said "What am I doing here in your house?"

I said "You don't remember?"

She said "Remember what?"

There was not one mark on her. This is the girl that had broken her arm, but she wouldn't believe me when I told her about it. I talked to Regina for about a week, trying to get her to stay there at the house. Regina would never have anything to do with what her mother and I were doing. She hated us for what we were doing. She just hated us, and she wouldn't talk to us.

> We just served her in love. And she resented it.

After she had left home twelve years earlier, she married a recently divorced man. Their lives had become this mess. We paid her rent, went to her house, cleaned her house, and took care of her baby. We just served her in love. And she resented it. She hated us.

Regina's husband used to bring his girlfriend to the house, and she wouldn't get out of the car.

We'd go out and say "Brenda, why can't you come in the house?"

She'd say "I could never come in your house."

I would say "Why?"

She would say, "Regina's in there."

I'd ask, "What's wrong with Regina? Regina loves you."

We eventually got Brenda to come in our house and bring her children in. We never judged what she was doing. We just loved all of them. If they were going to change, they would have to make a choice with the help of the Holy Spirit.

There is a war going on between Christians and the devil. Satan hates it when we serve God with love. Satan fills people with hatred and makes people depressed.

After the episode with Regina's broken arm, she got up at night and growled at us while she walked the halls. She was totally out of control. Jeanne and I would just pray for her. We never challenged her. We never told her, "You really need to see what you're doing to yourself." All we ever did was ask her, "Is there any way we can serve you? What can we do to help you today?"

Do you know how she responded?

"Growwwwwl."

One evening about three years later, she was standing in my doorway. I was sitting in my chair, I looked at her, and these words came out my mouth. "Regina, when was the last time you had a good thought about yourself?"

She said "I don't remember."

I said "Would you let me say some good things about you?"

She said "There aren't any."

I said "Oh, yes there are."

She said "What are they?"

I said "Do you know that you're unique, and you're special? Do you know that you're a gift from God? Do you know that when God created you, he created you out of love? God loves you!"

And it healed her—POW! It wasn't praying for her, it wasn't calling on the power of God's Holy Spirit. It was ministering the truth in love to her. She came out of a twelve-year depression, just like that.

> "Do you know that you're a gift from God? God loves you!"

During that time, Jeanne's father was in the hospital with colon cancer. They had just closed him back up after surgery, because they couldn't do anything for it. He was 90 years old. We brought him home, and a day care nurse came by to take care of him.

I told Regina, "You've got a special gift. You've got a special job. And you'll never know it until you allow this love that God has for you to come in."

So, Regina found out that her grandfather was sick, and she went in the other room to see him. The day nurse was there waiting on him, snatching the sheets out from under him.

Regina just went over and said "This is my Papa, and you can't treat him like that." Regina just started changing his bedding herself.

So, Regina began to take care of her grandfather. She'd change his colostomy bag. She'd change his urinal track. She'd bathe him, she'd change his clothes, and she'd change his sheets.

And he started saying to her, "Regina, you're much better than those nurses that wait on me. Are you going to be a nurse? I think you're going to be a nurse. I think I see you in a white uniform."

Regina has a great love for old people. She loves to wait on them. She could very easily be a geriatrics doctor. She's just that smart. We never knew she was smart. She's brilliant. She went through nursing school and got a scholarship in the last year. Her grades were so good that she got the first scholarship ever given out by her college for the course that she went through. And she eventually graduated from nursing school. Even though she never finished high school, she became a registered nurse. And she lost about 240 pounds.

Regina used to say "Dad, you live in a fantasy world."

I would say, "That's right—I live in a fantasy world—I don't live in this stinking, old, rotten world out here anymore. I live in a fantasy world. It's called the world of faith."

> **"I live in a fantasy world. It's called the world of faith."**

Thank God we're all saved by grace. I have been able to leave my kids alone and just love them. And I've found out that's the medicine, the power that brings conversion—not only to yourself but to the ones you're with. Once they realize that you just take them the way they are, they're able to change. They're able to bring about change in themselves. To me, that's genuine salvation.

Our society is geared to teach people that they're bad. It tells them that they're ugly, they don't fit, they're not acceptable, they need to change, they need to do this, they need to do that. I tell people that God loves us where we are.

One by one, the Osburn children came to the Lord. Each had obstacles to overcome, walls to tear down, and grief to suffer. But Jeanne and I had learned the lesson about love, and the Lord was faithful. We were patient and kind with our children. We never took offense at the things they did or said. We stood by them and helped them. Whenever they needed anything, we gave it to them. And that, according to God's holy word, is what love is all about.

CHAPTER TEN

# The Remedy for Fear

## Charlie Faces His Fears

When I was first learning how to love like a Christian, Father Smith also taught me never to compromise the word of God. He said, "Live the word and preach the word. Don't ever try to please people. Preach the truth, and let the Holy Spirit convict your listeners."

It wasn't always easy to remember Father Smith's words. When I first began to preach, I experienced a great deal of rejection, and I didn't like it. After we feel rejected enough times, we begin to fear it. Eventually, we are afraid to speak about the Lord.

All I wanted to do was live like Jesus when I took the prices off my menu. Everybody got mad at me. The county commissioners got upset at me. All I was doing was giving away food. They thought I was going over the edge. Later, I wondered, *what do the bishops think about me?*

At one point during my ministry, I had spent six months in the San Antonio diocese, preaching to the Catholic prayer groups there. In all that time, I had not met the archbishop. Then, one day I was told that he wanted to see me in his office. By the time I arrived, I was very nervous. I had never been called in by an archbishop before.

When I walked into his office, he looked up from his work and said, "So, you're Charlie Osburn."

"Yes," I said.

"I've heard many good things about you," he said.

At that statement, I breathed a tremendous, but silent, sigh of relief.

In the next breath, the archbishop said, "I've also heard some bad things. Sit down."

In an instant, my relief turned to terror. I had no idea what he was going to say. I knew that people were getting excited about the church because of my preaching. I knew that people were experiencing physical healing, and marriages were being reconciled. But I had no idea how an archbishop would receive all this.

> **In an instant, my relief turned to terror.**

"You know, Charlie," the archbishop continued, "I was raised on a farm down in southern Texas near the Mexican border. My father talked to me about Jesus from the time I was a small boy. One of the things he said stuck with me, and it applies to you. My father said, 'You can always identify a man of God by the reports that come after him. There will always be two reports—a good report and a bad report. There will be people healed, and there will be skeptics. Some people will encounter him and come away spiritually blessed. Others will condemn him.'"

The archbishop paused. "I've heard two reports about you, Charlie. Welcome to my diocese. Is there anything I can do for you?"

The meeting with the archbishop was a great turning point in my life. From that moment on, I knew that I didn't need to be afraid of what people think of me. If I preach the word in total submission to the bishop that God has placed over me, and if I live what I preach, the Lord will do everything else. There will always be a good report and a bad report, but God doesn't want me to be concerned about it.

This discovery liberated me and enabled me to move forward with my ministry, leaving the worry to God and the authority to those he has placed over me.

> **Fear is the biggest obstacle we face in sharing the good news.**

Fear is the biggest obstacle we face in sharing the good news. The remedy for that fear is to identify it and get rid of it.

Fear came into the world when Adam and Eve first sinned in the Garden of Eden. In Genesis 3:8–10, we read,

> Then the man and his wife heard the sound of the Lord God as he was walking in the garden in the cool of the day, and they hid from the Lord God among the trees of the garden. But the Lord

God called to the man, "Where are you?" He answered, "I heard you in the garden, and I was afraid because I was naked; so I hid."

Adam was afraid, because he knew that what he had done had separated him from God. He knew there was no hope for him. Now, he would live under the rule and power of Satan, and eventually, he would die. As he realized all these things, fear crept over him. That fear has reigned over all mankind ever since.

Fortunately, God was not content to leave things in such a state. The Bible tells us in Romans 5:17–18,

> For if, by the trespass of the one man (Adam), death reigned through that one man, how much more will those who receive God's abundant provision of grace and of the gift of righteousness reign in life through the one man, Jesus Christ. Consequently, just as the result of one trespass was condemnation for all men, so also the result of one act of righteousness was justification that brings life for all men.

We don't need to be afraid anymore. The sin of Adam and Eve brought fear into the world, but the victory of Jesus—his death and resurrection—eliminated the cause of fear. Jesus defeated Satan, the father of fear, and vanquished death forever. The Bible tells us that in Christ, there is no more death. We are going to live forever. In Christ, we have the joy of knowing that we are on the way to eternal glory. We will wear crowns and live with Jesus forever. There is nothing to fear.

> **Jesus defeated Satan. There is nothing to fear.**

I was once leading a meeting in California when I noticed a crippled woman walk in, hunched over a cane. It took her about fifteen minutes to get into a chair, and then she sat there shaking.

My subject that night was fear, and when I finished speaking, the woman came up to me and said, "I am scared to death."

"I can tell," I said. "You're about ready to die, aren't you, sister?"

She nodded her head and said, "I am."

"Well," I said, "We are going to get rid of that fear."

Then I prayed, "Satan, in the name of Jesus Christ who defeated you and cast out your fear, I command you to loose your hold of fear on my sister. Get away from her right now."

Immediately, she threw down her cane, straightened up, and walked out the door, exclaiming, "Hallelujah!"

Fear had crippled her inside and out. But when she heard the truth about Jesus, she believed and allowed him to drive fear out of her life.

Many of us are crippled internally, if not externally, by fear. We are afraid of the dark. We are afraid of criminals. We are afraid of losing our money. We are afraid of failure. Worst of all, we may be afraid that others will ridicule us if we live like Christians, so we hide our Christian faith under a bushel basket.

We don't have to live with our fears! Jesus has poured so much love into our lives through his life, his teaching, his death, and his resurrection. He has eliminated the need to be afraid. He has loved us with a perfect, everlasting love. We can read in I John 4:18, "There is no fear in love. But perfect love drives out fear, because fear has to do with punishment. The one who fears is not made perfect in love."

Jeanne was fearful about the idea of my learning how to fly. Whenever I got behind the wheel of a car, I had always fallen asleep within ten minutes. So, Jeanne drove whenever we went anywhere. She was afraid that if I flew a plane, I would fall asleep, just like I did when I drove.

After I got my pilot's license, Jeanne finally decided to fly with me on a trip to Shreveport. On that flight, we took along our granddaughter and Hilda Wheelis.

When we got over Mississippi, we ran into a bad thunderstorm. I wasn't an instrument-rated pilot yet, and I could barely see. Jeanne begged me to turn around. I had never been one to turn around once I made up my mind that I was going somewhere, so I kept flying headlong into that storm.

Well, Hilda began praying in tongues, and so did Jeanne. I figured, *this may be the last trip they ever take with me if I scare them. I'd better turn back.*

As soon as I turned, I got vertigo. The plane went into what is known as a dead man's spin: an upside-down spiral.

Isaiah 13:7–8 says, " . . . all hands will go limp, every man's heart will melt. Terror will seize them . . . " I experienced that day the kind of terror that makes your hands go limp. I couldn't move a muscle. My heart stopped, and my mind froze. I could not think of anything but impending death.

Then, I began to hear from the back Jeanne and Hilda praying in tongues. I began to pray in tongues, too. Suddenly, I heard the voice of my flight instructor: "Pull the power off, and turn loose the controls."

The paralysis that had gripped me ended. I pulled off the power and let go of the controls. It was contrary to everything that was natural for a man to do in that situation. In life, letting go of the controls is difficult for all of us. We don't want to let God take control of our hearts, either.

At 2,000 feet, an opening appeared in the clouds, and the plane came out of its downward spiral. I leveled off and flew without incident the rest of the way into Shreveport. After we landed, I got out to check the plane for damage. I figured we must have taken some heavy hits from hail. Surely the wings would be messed up.

There was not one mark on that plane. No hail damage. Nothing. I know that praying in tongues is not to be interpreted, but on that day, I asked, "Lord, what exactly was I saying to you up there?"

He said, "You were hollering 'Help!' and I heard your cry."

Several times while piloting an airplane since then, I have encountered mechanical failures and sudden, violent weather. If I had not known that Jesus' love has cast fear out of my life, I would have panicked. I would have allowed fear to grip my heart. Fear would have frozen my mind and kept my hands from doing what they needed to do to get me through the situation. But the Lord showed me that he is in control, and I do not need to be afraid.

> **The Lord showed me that he is in control.**

On another flight, I was heading home at about three o'clock in the morning over Lake Ponchartrain. I was completely alone, and as Jeanne had so often worried, I fell asleep at the controls. There was no auto pilot, just a wing leveler.

All of a sudden, somebody punched me in the back really hard. It scared the stew out of me, and I was wide awake. I looked down at the instrument panel, and looked up at the horizon. I was flying at 1,000 feet, just above the surface of the lake. I quickly pulled back up, and said a prayer of thanks. I knew the Holy Spirit saved me from fear that night.

I thought my job for years was to be wealthy and well liked. When I got there, it was empty. Now, my life is exciting. I am committed to serving the Catholic Church as a lay evangelist, fearlessly telling others about the love of Jesus.

We must be on the lookout for occasions to be a witness for Jesus. If we've never fallen in love with him, we'll never be able to tell anybody about him. If you are a man, think about when you first met your wife. The excitement of showing her around was really something, wasn't it? You felt like a macho man. You had a love that was exciting.

> **We must be on the lookout for occasions to be a witness for Jesus.**

Jesus is the center of all love. When we experience him and have a personal relationship with him, there's no reason to be afraid to share him with other people. We can say he's my brother, he's my Savior, my deliverer, my comfort, my joy, my enthusiasm, my excitement, my everything. I can't wait to share him!

Whether it's with one person or 100,000 people, I'm no longer afraid to share Jesus. I can't say that that was always the case.

One afternoon, I was in a real rush to get to an airport in Louisiana, because I had a speaking engagement later that evening. I was running late, and my car broke down on the way there. I prayed over the engine, and nothing happened.

I suddenly realized that I should be concerned in that place about why that car had broken down. I asked, "Lord, do you have a mechanic here that needs to be saved?"

God said, "Yes."

I went over to a phone booth and started thumbing through the yellow pages. *I'll take the closest garage.*

I called, and a big, old rough voice answered, "Yeah."

I said, "Will you send somebody to find out what's wrong with my car?"

Well, a while later, this great, big, old burly guy got out of the truck. Man, he was huge. He was greasy all over.

I said, "God, what on earth do you want me to talk to him for? He'll smoosh me out if I try to talk to him."

The Lord said, "He needs healing. Start talking."

He got down under my hood and began taking the alternator out.

I swallowed hard and said, "Do you know Jesus loves you?"

He raised up real quick and banged his bald head on the hood. He growled, "How do you know?"

The only thing I could think to say was, "He loves you, because he loves me."

He said, "Yeah, I know. If he loves you, he loves me." He wasn't buying it.

I took a deep breath and tried again. "Brother, is there something in your life that I could pray with you about? Is there a problem in your life? That's the reason you're here fixing my car. God wants me to pray for you so he can heal you."

He scowled at me and said, "How do you know?"

At that point, the Holy Spirit started doing the talking. I said, "Because he healed me."

"God healed you?'

"He did."

"You think he can heal me?"

I said, "He loves you, brother, as much as he loves anybody in the world."

"Are you sure?"

"I'm positive."

> **The Holy Spirit started doing the talking.**

All this time, he was still working on the car. I asked him as he got down under the hood again, "Would you like to give your life to Jesus?"

He turned his head, and great big tears were running from his eyes. "You know," he said, "nobody's ever asked me that before."

I just reached over and laid my hands on his bald old head. And I said, "Lord Jesus, my wonderful brother wants to turn his life over to you—Don't you brother?"

And he said, "Yes."

"My wonderful brother wants to receive the power of the Holy Spirit—Don't you brother?"

And he said, "Yes."

And I said, "Father, in Jesus' holy name, we thank you now for healing him of sugar diabetes. Father God, we claim this in faith. In Jesus' holy name we pray. Amen."

And that precious brother turned and looked at me and said, "What church do you go to?"

"The Holy Church," I said, "The Catholic Church."

He reared back and hollered, "What? How long you been a Catholic?"

I said, "Since I met Jesus."

Now let me explain something. In northern Pensacola, there were a lot of racially prejudiced people at that time. Only about five percent of us in Florida, Louisiana, Alabama, or Mississippi were Catholic. This guy began to tell me about his relationship with the Ku Klux Klan and how he hated the Blacks and how he hated the Mexicans and how he hated the government. Apparently, he hated Catholics, too.

I said, "No wonder you've got sugar diabetes. You've got the same problem I had. It's hate. Brother, don't you realize God didn't make any junk? You are one of the finest things God ever created."

He said, "Really?"

I said, "Yeah."

That day, when the car finally got fixed and I got done talking to him, that brother was healed and had a totally different outlook on life. He wasn't afraid to tell everybody he knew that a Catholic had led him to the Lord.

> **"You are one of the finest things God ever created."**

We can't just go to Mass for forty-five minutes every Sunday. We can't say, "Don't bother me until next week, and I'll come again." I tried sitting in the comfort of the pew for years and years, and it just about killed me. We must get up out of that pew and tell others what Jesus has done for us. We can lead people into the kingdom of God, because we have the help of the Holy Spirit. Bringing others into God's wonderful church is our duty, and we can rejoice in knowing that there is nothing to fear as we do.

---

**Peter Addresses the Crowd**

[14]Then Peter stood up with the Eleven, raised his voice and addressed the crowd: "Fellow Jews and all of you who live in Jerusalem, let me explain this to you; listen carefully to what I say. [15]These men are not drunk, as you suppose. It's only nine in the morning! [16]No, this is what was spoken by the prophet Joel:

[17]" 'In the last days, God says,
    I will pour out my Spirit on all people.
Your sons and daughters will prophesy,
    your young men will see visions,
    your old men will dream dreams.
[18]Even on my servants, both men and women,
    I will pour out my Spirit in those days,
    and they will prophesy.
[21]And everyone who calls
    on the name of the Lord will be saved.' . . ."

**Acts 2:14–18, 21**

## CHAPTER ELEVEN

# A Change in Plans

## Charlie Meets Some Adversity

Many young people entering the ministry today give up very quickly because they are afraid. They have been criticized and discouraged in their efforts to share the good news of Jesus Christ with the world. I want them to know that, even if they give up, God does not. He has a plan to help many people become lay evangelists, and he will continue working long after we quit.

Over the years, God showed me through two dreams and one vision that he had a plan to use me as a lay evangelist to teach others how to do what I do. Shortly after I was saved and while I was studying with the diaconate, I had a vivid dream. I was standing before a sea of people. I could not see the front or the back of the crowd. There was no end to either side of this vast assembly of men and women.

There was a guy standing next to me, and he said, "You're going to start a school for Christian evangelists."

I felt overwhelmed by this task, and I said, "I don't know anything about starting a school."

He said, "You didn't know anything before I showed it to you."

I went to Father Smith and told him about my dream.

Father Smith said, "You have to tell Bishop Lorenzo about this."

So, I flew to Tallahassee to see Bishop Lorenzo. He met me at the airport.

I said, "I had an unusual dream." I filled in the details and finished with, "I couldn't see an end to all of those people. What am I supposed to do?"

He looked at me and said, "The Holy Spirit has already told you what to do. Why are you asking me? Go back and start your school."

Some time later, I had a second dream. This time, I found myself in a vast desert, and I was standing on an oasis near a tent. There was a war going on nearby, and people began to come to this oasis from battle. They were badly wounded—bandaged, on crutches, and in wheelchairs.

The wounded people walked through the water of this oasis, and when they went out the other side, they were healed. From there, I sent each one back into battle, saying, "You gotta go back!"

I have already mentioned the vision that I had while I was cooking at our restaurant. I was taken into a heavenly realm, and I was looking down on the universe. I could see all of the stars, the galaxies, and the depth, beauty, and overwhelming immensity of God's creation.

The same guy who had spoken to me in my first dream said, "Charlie, I had you in mind when I built everything that you can see. If you had been the only one on earth, I would have made it just for you."

I was speechless.

He continued, "Don't you think I could run your restaurant? Don't you think I could run your life?"

God showed me through that vision that he could love me and help me move forward through all of life's challenges. I didn't need to be afraid, because God was in control. He could even help me start a School of Evangelization.

> **The whole world was excited about this School of Evangelization.**

These dreams and a vision motivated me to speak fearlessly to everyone I met about God's plan to open a School of Evangelization. I traveled to every state, Canada, the Philippines, and Central America, telling everyone what I wanted to do. The whole world was excited about this School of Evangelization.

I kept talking so much about my dreams that Bishop Marshall's news reporter from the *Florida Catholic*—our diocese's newspaper—kept coming to my office and asking me, "Charlie, when are you going to open that school?"

"Right away," I said one day.

I began looking for a building that we could use. I found an abandoned bar on Highway 98 that had been called The Old Corral.

The reporter took a picture of the building, and he submitted the story to the *Florida Catholic*. It made the front page, and the caption under the picture read, 'Future Home for Catholic School of Evangelization.'

When Bishop Marshall saw the newspaper, he called me and said, "God forbid that you could put a school in that building."

Bishop Marshall met me later at an old school called St. Anthony's. It was in a poor neighborhood, was drug-infested, and the windows were all broken out. At one time, it had been a segregated school for Black children, but it had been converted to some sort of a storage place. It was a mess. The bishop told me that the diocese would lease us the building so that we could use it for our school.

It was a historical day when Bishop Marshall later signed a ten-year lease on that vacant school building to allow our School of Evangelization to open. The lease was made between the diocese and Good News Ministries. We agreed to pay $1,000 a month, with a $50 per month increase every year.

It took us nearly one year to get the building cleaned up, and we spent about $100,000 replacing all of the windows. But on June 6, 1988, our first class opened to students from the United States, Canada, Central America, Africa, and many other countries. There were 150 people there to learn how to become lay evangelists.

At first, we planned for the classes to run for six weeks. We realized, though, that we couldn't expect people to leave their jobs and families for that long. So, we whittled it down to two weeks for that first session. Eventually, we fit the program into one week of classes.

The people in that first class were so excited about what we were doing, that some of them never left. They became janitors, office workers, cooks, and servants. For ten wonderful years, we taught people from all over the world how to use their faith to love others into the kingdom of God.

■ α ■

**We taught people from all over the world how to use their faith to love others into the kingdom of God.**

■ Ω ■

I told you earlier about my dreams. I realized after the School of Evangelization opened that God had fulfilled his plan. Those people in my second dream—the ones at the oasis—represented all of the students who came to our school. People came to us who were wounded, distressed, angry, and frustrated. We turned them around and sent them out with a different attitude, ready to battle the world with love.

Our school grew so large that we felt we needed some help. We had sixty-five people on staff, and we wanted someone to train them to better understand the current teachings that were going on at the seminaries. We wanted more information that we could pass on to our students.

I called one of the leading evangelists in the world at that time. He told me that he would send Father Enrico to help us.

When Father Enrico arrived, Jeanne and I took him to dinner.

He sat across the table from us and said, "I've come as an angel of light to destroy you."

I looked at my wife and said, "What did he say, Jeanne? I don't think I heard him right."

She said, "I don't know."

I looked at Father Enrico and said, "What did you say?"

He said again, "I've come as an angel of light to destroy you."

I couldn't believe what was coming out of his mouth. I said, "Well, if you can destroy the love that I've got inside me, then that love is no good. Take your best shot."

> **"If you can destroy the love that I've got inside me, then that love is no good."**

Over the next three months, Father Enrico worked behind my back to convince my students, our parish priest, and our staff that I wasn't teaching the whole truth.

I said to him at one point, "Tell me what I'm missing, and I'll be glad to teach it. But, I'm not sure that anyone understands everything, except Jesus."

One day, I got a call from the bishop in Belize to build a school and a place for missionaries there. Over the weekend while I was in Belize discussing this plan with the bishop there, Father Enrico met with Bishop Jones of our diocese in Florida. He took with him another priest named Father Steel, several laymen including a man named Mr. Frost, and members of our staff. They told Bishop Jones that they wanted me removed from the ministry.

When I returned from Belize, Father Enrico called me to a meeting. Bishop Jones, Father Steel, Mr. Frost, and several lay people were present.

Father Steel said, "We've been to talk to Bishop Jones. We asked him to have you removed from this ministry."

Bishop Jones said, "I don't feel comfortable discussing this without the Vicar General."

So, the Vicar General joined the meeting. Apparently, Father Enrico had preached at the Vicar General's church during the prior week, attempting to further undermine my ministry.

During the course of the meeting, this group of people tore me apart while Bishop Jones and the Vicar General listened. Father Enrico claimed that he had already succeeded in having me removed from the ministry.

Bishop Jones interrupted and said, "But I like what Charlie is doing." He turned to the Vicar General and said, "What are your feelings?"

The Vicar General said, "After what I have heard, I would never invite Father Enrico back to my church."

Bishop Jones turned to Father Enrico and said, "Where are you from?"

Father Enrico said, "New York."

Bishop Jones said, "Why don't you go back to New York and leave Charlie alone?"

Well, the Catholic Church never likes it when people begin to stir up trouble like Father Enrico did. The Vicar General disagreed with the whole mess, but he advised me to close the School of Evangelization.

After ten years of sending people out as lay evangelists, we closed our school in 1998. One week later, Mr. Frost, the man who had worked together with Father Enrico to shut us down, dropped dead.

> ■ α ■
> **The Vicar General advised me to close the School of Evangelization.**
> ■ Ω ■

I knew that these men could not stop the plans that God had put in place. He had given me my dreams and fulfilled my vision of sending people into the world as lay evangelists. God would find another way to make our dreams a reality.

**Unity in the Body of Christ**
¹As a prisoner for the Lord, then, I urge you to live a life worthy of the calling you have received. ²Be completely humble and gentle; be patient, bearing with one another in love. ³Make every effort to keep the unity of the Spirit through the bond of peace. ⁴There is one body and one Spirit—just as you were called to one hope when you were called— ⁵one Lord, one faith, one baptism; ⁶one God and Father of all, who is over all and through all and in all.

⁷But to each one of us grace has been given as Christ apportioned it. ⁸This is why it says:
"When he ascended on high,
he led captives in his train
and gave gifts to men."
⁹(What does "he ascended" mean except that he also descended to the lower, earthly regions? ¹⁰He who descended is the very one who ascended higher than all the heavens, in order to fill the whole universe.) ¹¹It was he who gave some to be apostles, some to be prophets, some to be evangelists, and some to be pastors and teachers, ¹²to prepare God's people for works of service, so that the body of Christ may be built up ¹³until we all reach unity in the faith and in the knowledge of the Son of God and become mature, attaining to the whole measure of the fullness of Christ.

¹⁴Then we will no longer be infants, tossed back and forth by the waves, and blown here and there by every wind of teaching and by the cunning and craftiness of men in their deceitful scheming. ¹⁵Instead, speaking the truth in love, we will in all things grow up into him who is the Head, that is, Christ. ¹⁶From him the whole body, joined and held together by every supporting ligament, grows and builds itself up in love, as each part does its work.

²⁹Do not let any unwholesome talk come out of your mouths, but only what is helpful for building others up according to their needs, that it may benefit those who listen. ³⁰And do not grieve the Holy Spirit of God, with whom you were sealed for the day of redemption. ³¹Get rid of all bitterness, rage and anger, brawling and slander, along with every form of malice. ³²Be kind and compassionate to one another, forgiving each other, just as in Christ God forgave you.

**Ephesians 4:1–16, 29–32**

CHAPTER TWELVE

# A New Mission From God

## Charlie Dreams of a School in Central America

In the same week that our school closed, I began working toward the goal of building the church and mission in Belize. Right away, it became clear that God wasn't going to quit on my dream of teaching our School of Evangelization. Neither was I. If I couldn't do it in Pensacola, I'd teach in Central America.

When I left Pensacola and I first got off the airplane in Belize, I rode in a car from the airport to the Cathedral. There is a river that runs all the way from the airport right in front of the Cathedral. A whole new thing happened to me when I arrived. I became like that water—Living Water was flowing out of me. I felt that God was making it clear about what we were supposed to do next.

> ■ α ■
> **I felt that God was making it clear about what we were supposed to do next.**
> ■ Ω ■

I was preaching in the Cathedral after I first arrived, but at the time I had not yet met Bishop Robin. I was preaching to the congregation, saying, "Do you believe that there is only one true God?"

The people mumbled, "Yes."

I said, "You sure don't sound very excited about it."

I said, "We believe in one God—the God who would make something white, who would make something black, something yellow, something brown. Do we believe that God is only one? Then why are we prejudiced? Why are we angry? Why are we frustrated? Why are we bitter and full of hate?"

A little Black guy at the back of the congregation shouted, "Amen!"

Throughout my whole talk, he shouted, "Praise the Lord!"

I asked, "Do you all really believe that Jesus Christ is true God and true Savior? How many have accepted him as Lord? Have you ever asked him to be the Lord of your life? Or do you just mimic these words?"

Someone jumped up and said, "My God, I am glad you are here. I have been waiting to do this all of my life! Jesus is the Lord of my Life!"

That evening, the people from the church took me into the reception hall. They said, "Would you like to meet Bishop Robin?"

I said, "Oh, I sure would."

Well, he ended up being that little Black guy who had been shouting from the back of the church, "Amen!"

Bishop Robin said, "I need help. Will you come and help? I haven't had anybody explain my faith like you have. You are a visionary."

I said, "Well, I don't know about that, but I have a tremendous love for people."

■ α ■

**"I want you to build our church in Buttonwood Bay."**

■ Ω ■

Bishop Robin talked to Jeanne and me a short time later. He said, "You're a teacher of faith. I need you to teach my people how to love. We have been praying for seventy-five years for someone to help us build a parish church. I want you to build our church in Buttonwood Bay. It is a very small village in a remote area. You will be in charge of the spirituality of that church."

When the bishop asked for a building, I said to him. "We'll see if we can build a church."

Bishop Robin said, "I've got something better than that. I'm going to give you a church."

I said to Jeanne, "Honey, did you hear that?"

He said, "Well, I'm not giving you the building, but I am giving you a place to build it. You are going to oversee the construction of a church. I want you to get an architect. I want you to go tell the people in the community that you are going to build them a church."

Well, we left Belize on a Friday, and I flew to New Jersey on Saturday night. I spoke to a group of ladies on Sunday morning at a

Holy Rosary service, and I mentioned the fact that the bishop wanted a center of evangelization built in Central America for the world.

I said, "We are going to train evangelists there to send out all over the world."

On Monday morning, when I started our classes, this lady rushed in and said, "I want to see you outside."

Now I had never seen her before. The only thing that I can think of is that she had to have been at that Holy Rosary service on Sunday morning.

She said, "God is telling me to do this, and I have to do it before I change my mind."

She handed me a check for $100,000. That was three days after God had told me to build a church in Belize.

I called Bishop Robin and said, "We are definitely going to build a church."

Every time we would get to a dead-end in the process of building our church and felt that we could not go any further, a Christ 'happening' would take place. Things happened to us in Belize that nobody would believe. Total strangers that we did not even know—people who had heard one of our tapes ten years earlier—would call us to donate incredible sums of money: $50,000, $100,000, $200,000.

One would say, "You know, God has really impressed on me to donate!"

Another person would call, saying, "You don't even know me. My mother gave me this tape ten years ago. I listened to it every day for ten years. It has saved my life so many times." That is what built our ministry: the Word of God and the power of his Holy Spirit. We raised $400,000 in just a few months for our new church in Buttonwood Bay.

> ■ α ■
> **That is what built our ministry: the Word of God and the power of his Holy Spirit.**
> ■ Ω ■

Nobody got together to plan how we were going to build the church. There was nothing there but the Holy Spirit and people walking the streets looking for work. Immigrants from other countries came to build the church. They became our church family.

One day, I was in town getting my hair cut at the barber shop. Nobody knew me there in Belize.

My daughter said to a girl in the shop, "This is my dad."

This little girl said, "Is he Charlie Osburn?"

My daughter said, "Yes, he is."

The girl said that her friend had been praying for God to help her. She did not know who to turn to or what to do. She came out of her house in the morning to find that someone from the house next door had dumped their garbage out. There were a lot of books in a pile. She felt compelled to look through those books, and she saw *The Charlie Osburn Story*. Through that book, she had given her life to Jesus. That is just one story about overcoming suffering that we have heard.

I tell people that suffering purifies the soul. It is in our suffering that we cry out. If we had everything just the way we wanted it, then we wouldn't need God. When everything gets tough, we get upset and cry out to God. When we are crying out to God, he hears us. Everything is in place for him to talk to us. No matter where we are in our circumstances, if we cry out to him, he has someone there to reach out to us.

I was speaking in the Cathedral one night, and I said to the crowd, "God is eager to show his love for us. He is intent to love us. I know there is someone here tonight who is really hurting. To show you how much he really loves you, I am not going to pray for you individually. We are all just going to lay hands on one another, and God is going to work through you to heal the person next to you."

There was a lady sitting there with a tumor on the end of her spine. She said that the minute the lady next to her laid hands on her, she felt it disappear. She later joined the church. Since then, she has experienced other things that most people think are phenomenal. They are not. They are simply part of the Lord's kingdom.

Jesus kept telling the people, "The kingdom is at hand."

Most people think that the kingdom Jesus was talking about was heaven. It is here now! The kingdom lives. In the Lord's Prayer we say, "Your kingdom come, your will be done on earth as it is in heaven." So, his kingdom is here, and his will is being done here like it is in heaven.

## Jeanne Remembers the People of Buttonwood Bay

Father Ramirez used to visit us and preach at the Cathedral in Belize. He was a young priest who was very short, but people were overwhelmed by him. He was just filled with the Holy Spirit. One Sunday, he flew in to have Mass with us at the Cathedral. We had chosen an opening song called 'Hallelujah, Sing to the Lord.' Father Ramirez came down the aisle, and the people were singing with absolutely no expression. He got down to the end of the aisle and jumped up on the front pew with all his robes on.

The people gasped.

He said, "This is the great jubilee! Do you know what jubilee means? It means joy! We have got to sing this song again."

Father Ramirez started singing the song over, and we must have sung 'Sing to the Lord' at least eight or ten times before he started the Mass. You could have heard us for blocks. He had those people so excited. They had never experienced anything like that in all their lives. People would have thought, *This just can't be a Catholic church!*

> ■ α ■
> **This just can't be a Catholic church!**
> ■ Ω ■

The people were so excited, they did not want to leave after that. They immediately fell in love with Father Ramirez.

People are hungry for the love and excitement and freedom that Father Ramirez taught. One of the nuns who taught in St. Catherine's Academy of Belize asked Father Ramirez if she could arrange to have all the kids come over to the Cathedral while he had Mass.

He said, "I would love it."

Well, at eight in the morning, buses started rolling down to the little church. We must have had six or eight hundred kids there, all in white uniforms with little ties.

The kids hadn't been there for the previous Mass on Sunday. While they were singing the opening song, Father Ramirez jumped up on the front pew again and said, "Now, let me tell you what you sound like."

Before it was all over, he had the kids smiling and clapping and shouting. They were shouting, "Hallelujah!" and raising their hands. The Mass went on for nearly two hours, and they did not want to leave.

The principal at the school asked the kids to write a journal on what happened, and the sister told us that the bulk of the journals said, "If we had Masses like that all the time, we would want to go to church."

> ■ α ■
> **"If we had Masses like that all the time, we would want to go to church."**
> ■ Ω ■

We hoped Father Ramirez would come back to Belize. He asked the archbishop if he could come and do missionary work with us, but the archbishop said that he really needed him elsewhere. I could see why. I'm hoping Father Ramirez will be a bishop someday. He was dynamite!

A while later, we went to Lorietta, New Mexico. Charlie was talking about the church in Buttonwood Bay. He told the people that it was almost finished and that he was going to live there. He told them that we were going to have the School of Evangelization every month for the year 2000. This is what the bishop had asked us to do.

When Charlie was through talking, he went to the back of the church.

I asked him, "Which priest is coming for the month of January?"

He said, "I don't know. Who do you think I should ask?"

I said, "You ought to bring Father Ramirez over. The people love him, and he is full of the Holy Spirit."

Father Ramirez was in his thirties, and he had a ponytail that came down to his waist. I was thinking when I told Charlie to invite him, *I wonder what the people will think about his ponytail?* Father Ramirez had received a lot of flack about it.

Before we left Lorietta, Father Ramirez agreed to preach in Belize in January.

■ α ■

**We dedicated our new parish church in 2000.**

■ Ω ■

He said, "I have something to tell you. Beginning in January of 2000, a new millennium, I am going to cut off my ponytail!"

So Father Ramirez ended up coming on his own, and sure enough, he showed up without his ponytail! He told us he had grown the ponytail so that when he started to go bald, he could throw it over his bald spot. He worked a lot with gangs in New Mexico, and I think his ponytail helped the kids to better identify with him. While Father Ramirez was visiting, we dedicated our new parish church in 2000, just in time for the new millennium. We named it the Divine Mercy Church of Buttonwood Bay.

CHAPTER THIRTEEN

# Help for the Hurting

## Charlie Tells About the People Who Were Helped

When I went down to live in Belize, Bishop Robin asked me, "When do you want to begin your ministry?"

I said, "Not until the building is finished."

When I first went to Buttonwood Bay, I really wasn't sure what I was going to do. I got up one morning after the building was finished and opened the front door of the church. I sat there, and I meditated and conversed with God. I said, "God, you know, you brought the people here to build this place. Now what do you want me to do?"

Within ten minutes, they started coming in.

About a month after the church building was finished, a lady from down the street called me up and said, "I really need help with my daughter. I need someone to talk to her."

I said, "I would be glad to talk to her."

The family came down, and I said, "Let me talk to your daughter first."

I asked her, "How are you angry?"

Boy, she let me have it!

I said, "Is anger a good spirit or a bad spirit?"

She said, "Oh, it's a bad spirit!"

I said, "You are entertaining a bad spirit. Would you like me to teach you how to get out of that attitude? If you will do something for the next sixty days, you will be free."

Two weeks later, her mother called me again and said, "She is right back into trouble again!"

That time, I went to her house. There were three girls there—the daughter and her two friends. I sat and talked with them for about an hour, and they asked me to come back.

I said, "Okay, I will be back on Friday."

We built the church. But more importantly, we needed to teach the people what that building represented. God allowed me to start with the youth. I had no clue that it would work like that—right when I finished the building.

> **God allowed me to start with the youth.**

The girl's mother told me about a month later that her daughter's whole attitude had changed. The youth could hear about the kingdom of God a lot better than adults could.

In Belize, the kids do not associate with the adults. Seventy-five percent of the population is over eighteen years old. When driving the streets around 7:30 in the morning, one can see thousands of young people are walking to school. At the same time, there are thousands who are not able to go to school, because there is no room for them. The schools are full.

The first two or three times I met with those kids, I had to force myself to go out with them. I was tired from working, and I really did not want to go. After a while, I couldn't wait. Eventually, they were all baptized in the Holy Spirit.

In that culture, the boys do not hang out with the girls, and the girls do not hang out with the boys. They do not have peer groups. It is hard for them to come together in a group.

One Friday night, the girl I had been talking to came up to me and said, "Would it be okay if some of the boys came to our meeting?"

I said, "It would fine."

About thirty minutes later, three guys showed up.

I told those guys, "Now look, I'm expecting to have as many guys here as girls. Now you guys go out and round them up."

By the fifth Friday, there were twenty-three kids in attendance, and it grew from there. That's when I realized why God had sent me to Buttonwood Bay. A lot of people needed our help.

> **A lot of people needed our help.**

Delano is a good example of an individual who needed our help. He could not read or write, but he could wire an entire building and finish the plumbing without ever looking at a plan. I think he was from El Salvador.

Delano talked about his dad once in a while, who lived in Texas. Americans frequently go down to places like Belize and have an affair with the local girls. Every woman there has an average of six children. It is almost like the biblical days in the Old Testament, where Abraham was married to Sarah, yet he had a concubine. That is very prominent in Belize. One man has a family here, and yet he has another one over there. He does not even give them his name. I don't know how they keep up. That is just how they do things there.

Another thing that we heard about when we first went to Belize was that incest was very common. We figured that sleeping in close quarters might have something to do with the problem.

Anyway, Delano was helping us build the church. He was paying $250 a month for a broken down flat that he was staying in. That is a lot of money for a migrant worker. When we went to his house to see where he lived . . . well, have you ever seen a dollhouse on stilts? That is what his place looked like. There were no beds or furniture. They slept on cardboard. When I walked in, his wife handed me a hot tortilla. I knew that was all they had.

> ■ α ■
> **When I walked in, his wife handed me a hot tortilla. I knew that was all they had.**
> ■ Ω ■

## Jeanne Compares the Central American Lifestyle to Ours

We had a little shed on the side of our building where we kept our concrete. As we were getting rid of the concrete and the shed was getting emptier and emptier, Delano asked Charlie what he was going to do with the shed. Charlie said, "I will probably tear it down. Why are you asking?"

He said, "I would like to know if I can move my family into it."

Charlie said, "Where do you live?"

He said, "Right now we are on the second floor of a building, and when the wind blows, I feel like it might fall down because it keeps swaying."

Charlie said, "Take me to where you live."

So I went with Charlie and this fellow in the car. I wouldn't even go up the steps, because I didn't think it would hold me.

After we arrived back at our place, the next thing I knew, I heard all this noise.

"Heave HO!"

I looked outside. Charlie was in this little Jeep. All the men that were working had tied a rope around that shed. The men pushed, and the Jeep pulled, as they manipulated it over to a piece of ground. That day, Delano went home and got his wife and two children, and they moved in.

Our utility shed back home was bigger than that one. It was so little that Charlie bought some lumber and made an extension to it. He also bought them a screen door and some fans for the inside. He hooked up electricity. They all slept on the floor. Charlie bought them a mattress to sleep on. For toiletries they came over to our mission and used the first floor shower. There were seven people altogether that lived in that shed. That was part of our missionary work.

■ α ■
**There were seven people altogether that lived in that shed.**
■ Ω ■

When people came to visit us in Buttonwood Bay, we told them how things were set up. Delano worked there, and his children were some of the ones being taught English by a couple from Albuquerque. A little girl had been so abused that Delano's family took her in. Her name was Brigitte, and she just loved us.

Charlie asked me one day, "Do you think you would like to adopt a child sometime?" Charlie felt really needed there at that time to help those people. Back in the states we had so much stuff, and so did our grandchildren. Those kids didn't have anything.

One day, Brigitte found a couple of empty boxes and put them on her feet. The boxes were like shoes. She went around playing and stomping in the dirt.

■ α ■
**Those kids have absolutely nothing, and yet they are so happy.**
■ Ω ■

Another day, she came and took some boards and ran home saying "Mama, Mama!" She built a see-saw and a slide out of those boards. Children in Belize don't have toys, just little cans or a mat, chickens and turkeys. The children like to play with the animals. It is amazing how selfish our children and grandchildren can be with everything that they have. Those kids have absolutely nothing, and yet they are so happy.

## Charlie Helps Delano's Family

Two months after we finished the shed, Delano's wife took off down south and brought two of her kids back with her. Six people lived in that shed, and it was only eighteen feet long. They were so excited about it.

Delano's wife was going through menopause, and her breast got really hard. She had some sort of viral infection. I told her to go see the doctor. They do have some good medical facilities in Belize. They ran a CAT scan and gave her some medicine. They said she was at high risk for breast cancer, and they wanted to check her every six months. We paid that bill for her.

For the first time in his life, Delano was able to help his mama. His mama was able to come and visit them from Oswald on the bus. He began building a shed nearby for her to live in.

Delano's wife cooked for six people on a one-burner kerosene stove. I hired both of her sons to work for our construction company, and Delano was the foreman of that little group. When they began making pretty good money, they began to think of other things besides the bare necessities. They went out and bought a butane three-burner stove. They were so excited! I was invited into their house to look at it.

## Jeanne is Frustrated by the Language Barrier

Charlie and I were together at a meeting with the church committee members one day, and Bishop Robin said, "I will match $15,000 if you can raise $15,000."

Later on, we were at a group meeting at a lady's house down the road, and a couple had come from Tennessee. It was a small group of husbands and wives. Charlie had told them what the bishop had said, and within minutes they had raised $15,000 by themselves.

Charlie went to Bishop Robin the next day and told him we had raised the money. The bishop was just shocked by what God could do! He was shocked by how fast a lot of things happened down there in Buttonwood Bay.

We needed the land next door to the church for a daycare center. Somehow, we had to pay for it.

The bishop said, "You must get that land, because it is valuable for the church." The bishop found out that the owner wanted to sell it for $200,000. He told Charlie, "You have got to buy it."

That land was once a nursery where they grew flowers. The owner told Charlie that he owned three nurseries in Belize. The other two were flourishing, but this one had never done well. Charlie felt that the Lord wasn't ever going to let anything grow there! He figured that the Lord had other plans for the land. We never had to worry about raising the money to buy the land, because the land owner donated his property to the church. It was absolutely wonderful, because it was near the main road going into town, and the view was beautiful.

Charlie really wanted to have a daycare center for the children. Everywhere you go in Belize, there are children roaming the streets. I was amazed at how they were all by themselves. Back in the States, very seldom do you see kids that are all by themselves like that. There, everything breaks at lunch time, and the kids go home. The kids are all very little—around kindergarten age—and you see them walking by themselves. So the bishop was very affirmative about a place for the children while the parents work.

So Charlie was hoping that it would not only be a daycare center, but also a place where we could board kids who have no place to go. It would be a boarding house, not an orphanage, because sometimes these people came back for their kids. We had a little girl living there, and one day the parents came back and took her home. Charlie figured that if parents could not take care of their children, they would at least have a place to leave them for a short while.

Shortly after the parish church opened in Buttonwood Bay, a man from the East Coast called and promised to donate $1 million to build a daycare center. As of this writing, he has not yet been able to follow through on that promise, but we feel certain that God is not finished with that plan yet.

■ α ■

**I felt so handicapped at times, and I tried to learn Spanish.**

■ Ω ■

The people who lost their homes in Honduras came by the mission and watched the work going on. Charlie hired them. They couldn't speak a word of English, and Charlie could not speak a word of Spanish. I felt so handicapped at times, and I tried to learn Spanish. All the folks from Albuquerque were fluent in Spanish. This is how some English classes all came about.

The people from Albuquerque started to teach the kids how to speak English. A man down the street had a classroom and a blackboard, and every morning they went down at ten o'clock. There were also some men who did not know how to speak English, and the people from Albuquerque taught them at night. We thought it would be very good if they could help start a daycare center, too. I can't say they came too early, because I think they needed to experience life over there. Everyone was where they needed to be at that time. Charlie loved it there. He loved the people, and he was very good with them.

We had people arrive at the mission with no money and no food. Charlie just gave to them whatever we had. Charlie is very free-hearted. We had people coming there with little kids who had no teeth left in their mouths.

They would hand us a note that read, "Will you help me?"

Charlie always helped them.

## Charlie's Heart Breaks for Needy People

In the United States, our poverty level was at about $12,000 a year in 2000. Over 80% of the people in Belize lived beneath the poverty level at that time. There are a few rich people there, and everyone else is poor. There is no middle class. This goes for the whole country.

Most of the people who came to the mission wouldn't tell me their real names. Many were illegal immigrants from other countries. We had a guy who worked for us who called himself Leroy Lincoln.

There was one worker who was put in jail. He was a young boy and a good worker from Nicaragua. There were so many wars going on there in Central America—El Salvador, Nicaragua, and Honduras. Honduras got wiped out by a hurricane in 2000. It destroyed 90% of the bridges in the country. The people were desperate. They were walking the streets looking for work. I finished building the church with people who had been run out of their countries.

During the day, I would talk to my workers—not at a specific time—whenever an opportunity arose. One day I went in, and the workers were having an argument. I said, "Hold it!"

They were bickering about one another's jobs.

Delano could speak English, so I asked him to interpret for me. I said, "Delano, ask him what his job is."

> **I finished building the church with people who had been run out of their countries.**

Delano asked the man in Spanish what his job was. He said he was a plasterer.

I said, "Delano, you tell him to get his plastering tools and get on that wall and plaster that wall and stop worrying about other people and what they are doing. It is none of his business."

I had nine guys working that day. I continued speaking to each one through Delano. I never had a problem with them arguing after that. This is how I taught the guys to work together and to have respect for one another.

After about seven or eight months, the men knew the work was running out. They said, "We don't want to leave you."

They moved into the church and slept there overnight—all nine of them.

> ■ α ■
> **We started the Good News Construction Company.**
> ■ Ω ■

I said, "Well, fellows I don't know what we are going to do. Maybe we can start a construction company." So, we started the Good News Construction Company.

There were others who also needed our help. When we used to travel a great deal, we had a lot of time on our hands, so we went fishing. Years ago, I met a guide who was working for a little marina known as Blue Water. We called him Sonny, and he would always take us fishing.

When I went to Belize to start the mission, I looked up Sonny. I said, "Sonny, do you need some fishing rods?"

"Sure," he said.

I bought all the fishing rods he could use to help him start his own business. We called it Good News Sports Fishing. After tourists caught the fish, Sonny would clean them so that they were ready to cook.

Across the border in Guatemala and Honduras, people lived under pieces of cardboard and plastic. I try not to get too emotional, because the poor will always be with us, but sometimes I was just overwhelmed by it all. I tried to help a few of them, too, as they came my way.

The Assemblies of God and Pentecostals have made a tremendous impact in Belize. One of the strong Christian communities there is the Mennonites. They own most of Belize. They are farmers. In fact, if it were not for the Mennonites, the people of Belize would starve to death.

Several years before this, I went to Tijuana to help people who were pouring in from El Salvador. Mother Teresa was there, comforting people who were physically dying. I was in awe, watching her at work. I helped where I could.

One day, a little guy ran up to Mother Teresa. He said, "We have food. We have water. You can see that we have shelter."

> **Mother Teresa was there, comforting people who were dying.**

I turned to look at their makeshift houses. They were living on pieces of cardboard with plastic tarps overhead.

The little boy shielded his eyes from the sun and said to Mother Teresa, "But we have no one to preach the gospel to us."

Mother Teresa just looked at me. She never said a word, but moved quietly among those who were dying.

It was very difficult for me, knowing that I couldn't speak Spanish. Very few of the people there would have been able to understand my message if I did share it with them. Still, that little boy inspired me. I couldn't conceive of how God could send his message of love to every person on the planet, but I knew that nothing is too big for him.

On another occasion, I visited a remote village in Africa. The people living there had been taught about Christianity by Catholic missionaries, but they were not living out their faith. They continued to kill each other in brutal wars between their tribes, just as they did hundreds of years ago.

A young priest traveled with me through the bush. We would stop under a tree, and I would begin to preach. He stood beside me with a megaphone, translating my message into the dialect of that region.

After two weeks of listening to my message, the young priest suddenly lowered his megaphone in the middle of my message and stopped translating. I wondered what was going on.

He looked at me and said, "Praise be to God!" He had received the baptism of the Holy Spirit. In the next moment, he began preaching directly to the people through his megaphone.

God calls all of us to help others who are in need. Some of us are called to far-away places such as Belize or Tijuana or Africa. But we don't have to go far to find people who need us. They live right in our own houses. There are others next door to us and across the street. We can all help those who need us if we are willing to open our hearts and pour out the love of Jesus into their lives.

### The Armor of God

¹⁰Finally, be strong in the Lord and in his mighty power. ¹¹Put on the full armor of God so that you can take your stand against the devil's schemes. ¹²For our struggle is not against flesh and blood, but against the rulers, against the authorities, against the powers of this dark world and against the spiritual forces of evil in the heavenly realms. ¹³Therefore put on the full armor of God, so that when the day of evil comes, you may be able to stand your ground, and after you have done everything, to stand. ¹⁴Stand firm then, with the belt of truth buckled around your waist, with the breastplate of righteousness in place, ¹⁵and with your feet fitted with the readiness that comes from the gospel of peace. ¹⁶In addition to all this, take up the shield of faith, with which you can extinguish all the flaming arrows of the evil one. ¹⁷Take the helmet of salvation and the sword of the Spirit, which is the word of God. ¹⁸And pray in the Spirit on all occasions with all kinds of prayers and requests. With this in mind, be alert and always keep on praying for all the saints.

**Ephesians 6:10–18**

CHAPTER FOURTEEN

# Lessons From Christ

## Charlie Reflects on What He Has Learned

It has been almost thirty years now since I have been in the ministry. I think I have picked up a little wisdom along the way. Here are some things I think about. Over the years, the most important point I have tried to communicate to people is that we must establish an intimate personal relationship with Jesus Christ. I have tried to teach people that we are a unique creation of God. Through the power of the Holy Spirit, we come in contact with the Lord and get saved.

> **We must establish an intimate personal relationship with Jesus Christ.**

We can see the effects of Jesus' life on the world. Jesus said we should give what we have to anybody who asks. All he had to give was himself—love, healing, patience, kindness, and generosity. This man never owned anything. He did not have a house to stay in. He told us, "Foxes have holes and birds of the air have nests, but the Son of Man has no place to lay his head." (Matthew 8:20) He lived wherever he could. I have done that for the past thirty years. I have lived wherever I could, so I began to see a little bit of what Jesus' life was like. Walking in his footsteps means living like he lived and talking like he talked.

I have seen many people trying to imitate rock stars and actors. This is tragic. Why is it so hard for us to think about imitating Jesus? We say we believe that Jesus is the Son of God, the only mediator between God and humans. It makes no sense to be lazy about praying or to feel sheepish about evangelizing.

When God called us to be Christ-like, he gave us the human model in the man, Jesus. We can love like he did. We can share the good news like he did. He was the greatest lay evangelist that ever lived!

I have learned that we must love our enemies. We must do good to those who hate us. That was something that became more than words to Jesus. They were his life. When they hung him on a cross, Jesus said, "Father, forgive them, for they know not what they are doing." (Luke 23:34) That is what love is. He did not condemn people, he forgave them.

I believe that salvation comes to us by doing things Jesus' way. In Luke 6:46 Jesus said, "Why do you call me 'Lord, Lord' and do not do what I say?" Remember, James 2:18 says, " . . . Show me your faith without deeds, and I will show you my faith by what I do." If we keep our faith to ourselves, it will not bring life to the people who need it.

> **We are one body, and we have one head—Jesus Christ.**

We are the church—the people of God who are baptized and confirmed and who assemble regularly to worship God and hear his word. The individual people—lay people, priests, bishops, and pope—are all the church. We are one body, and we have one head—Jesus Christ. Jesus is in charge.

All of us are holy. That means we have been set apart from the world for evangelization and good works. Each one of us has been given special gifts that no one else has. If we don't do the work that God has sent us to earth to do, it won't get done.

> **If we have faith in God, it will produce love.**

As apostles of Jesus Christ, we must act on our faith. We must proclaim Jesus Christ as Lord, loving one another with intense love. We have a role to win the world for Jesus through love.

I have learned that we must have faith in order to learn how to love. According to Galatians 5:22, faith empowers us to love. If we have faith in God, it will produce love.

I Corinthians 13:4–8 tells us what love looks like:

> Love is patient, love is kind. It does not envy, it does not boast, it is not proud. It is not rude, it is not self-seeking, it is not easily

angered, it keeps no record of wrongs. Love does not delight in evil but rejoices with the truth. It always protects, always trusts, always hopes, always perseveres. Love never fails.

Faith can be a great source of hope for Christians who desire church renewal, but are not seeing it in their local church. We should look not so much at what we see in our church, but at the unseen. We should envision the church as full of excited, enthused people on fire with the love and power of the Holy Spirit, doing the work God has called them to do. That's the way I look at the church—in the unseen. I haven't seen complete renewal yet, but I believe in it because it is God's plan for the church. He will bring it to pass.

God is a god of love. So faith produces love, and love becomes a sacrifice—for better or for worse. I love a person when they are good, and I love them when they are bad. I love them when they are sick, and I love them when they are well. I love them if they are rich, and I love them if they are poor. That is the attitude of Christ. It is an agape kind of love. For whatever reason, we adopted these ideas in our marriage vows. I think everybody should live those vows with all people. I should love others when they are behaving well and when they aren't. There are times when I behave well and times when I don't. Love is unconditional from my viewpoint. There are no conditions with love.

> **There are no conditions with love.**

Some people like to go back to the Old Testament law and say that God gets angry at people who aren't behaving well. In my opinion, the Old Testament people didn't know God. They had faith in God, but they did not know him. The God they knew was an angry God. God did not reveal himself until Jesus Christ was born. Most of the world today still lives with an angry God. The God I serve is a loving God. He is not an angry God. We are living under God's grace. It is time to embrace his mercy and distribute it to others.

> **It is time to embrace his mercy and distribute it to others.**

When we were baptized in Jesus Christ, our sins were forgiven. He freed us from the hold that sin had on our lives. We do not need to feel guilty any longer about our past sins. We can walk in holiness.

This does not mean that we will never sin again. It means that when we do, we can repent and receive forgiveness from God.

Others may argue that God can't be all that loving if he allows some people to go to hell for not accepting Christ. God gave us all free will. We can choose whatever we want. While we are here on earth, sins such as anger, frustration, resistance, hate, rebellion, greed, selfishness, arrogance, money, and envy separate us from God. We need to live in a spiritual place with God. We need to make a choice to have a personal relationship with Jesus Christ. And when we do, we will enjoy his peace, joy, and righteousness while we are here on earth, and when we get to heaven.

> ■ α ■
> **We can't walk past a person in need and say, "Praise the Lord!"**
> ■ Ω ■

I have found that I get more results in ministry just by sharing what I have with people. When people ask for something, we must give it if we can. We must see the needs of others. I John 3:17 says, "If anyone has material possessions and sees his brother in need but has not pity on him, how can the love of God be in him?" We can't walk past a person in need and say, "Praise the Lord! Have a great day! God bless you!" If we don't take care of the need, then the love of God can't be in our hearts.

I never cease to find exhilarating excitement in doing things for others. I will never forget the day that I pulled that little shed around for Delano's family to live in. Then again, I won't forget all the times that I thought that I was giving him second best. I felt that I was living in a penthouse while he lived in a shack.

Matthew 19:29 says, "And everyone who has left houses or brothers or sisters or father or mother or children or fields for my sake will receive a hundred times as much and will inherit eternal life." The Scriptures are clear that I may be getting my reward now, and Delano may be getting his later.

Sometimes I think that Delano may already be receiving some of his reward, due to his living conditions. He is patient with his family. He is not screaming that his needs must be met immediately. He is a hard worker, and he has all the fruits of the spirit.

I am doing a lot to help others, but I often feel that I am not doing enough. I like to share and work with people who need help. Belize is a desperate place. There is a refugee camp there. Americans ought to go through the camp or visit their prison. It is heartbreaking. We would not treat dogs in the U.S. the way they treat people down there.

They have twenty men stacked in a room the size of a small shed. They have no toilet—just a bucket. They throw it out of the cell and hose it down twice a day. You just can't imagine the inhumane treatment. Anybody walking into a situation like that can give great hope to those who are suffering.

Some people who have never been to places like Belize think that the poverty and the whole terrible situation is so overwhelming that there is no way to change any of it.

I have discovered that we can't change the situation, but God will use it to change us.

I have learned a lot, and through my experiences, God wants me to change. Sometimes the problem is not out there, the problem is in my head. The problem is in the way I perceive things. In Matthew 6:22, Jesus said,

> The eye is the lamp of the body. If your eyes are good, your whole body will be full of light. But if your eyes are bad, your whole body will be full of darkness. If then the light within you is darkness, how great is that darkness!

Some of these parables that Jesus taught used to drive me crazy. I wondered, *what is he talking about?* Jesus said in Matthew 5:29, "If your eye causes you to sin, gouge it out and throw it away." I came to realize that the eye doesn't see, the mind sees. The eye is an instrument that reflects light. My eye is a reflection of my mind. I can only see what has been perceived in my mind. My environment, my upbringing, my education have all changed my perception of others and the world around me. My eye sees with that in mind. What I have had to do is work on my mind, so that I see differently and take on the mind of Christ. This parable ought to be about cutting off my head, not about plucking out my eye.

I find my life much easier than it was in years past. I am getting to the point where if I see a problem with anything, I get to work on

> ■ α ■
> **We can't change the situation, but God will use it to change us.**
> ■ Ω ■

> ■ α ■
> **If I see a problem with you, then I get to work on changing me, not you!**
> ■ Ω ■

the problem in my mind. So, if I see a problem with you, then I get to work on changing me, not you!

As I have grown older, I have come to understand that God wants me to embrace my suffering, rather than fight it. I left Belize in 2001, because I wasn't feeling well. I didn't know what the problem was.

I prayed, "Oh God, this destroyed body is yours. You made it, now I put it into your care. I'm not going to fight it. I will embrace these symptoms, because I know you will be glorified. The Holy Spirit is in me, working to bring me closer to you. I thank you for these symptoms."

When I got back to the States, I got a call from my friend, Pete Wilson, who is a pharmacist. He wanted me to go out to El Centro, California, to present my School of Evangelization at a mission there.

When I got off the plane in California, Pete took one look at me and asked, "What's wrong, Charlie?"

I was moving really slow, and I said, "I'm just getting old. I'm nearly seventy now."

> ■ α ■
> **"You're a walking dead man."**
> ■ Ω ■

Pete said, "No, that's not the problem." We went back to his house, and he took my blood pressure. He looked up at me and said, "You're a walking dead man."

Pete wanted to call Dr. Howard Wayne, the author of the book, *How to Protect Your Heart from Your Doctor*. This guy was famous, and the odds of getting in to see him were about nine million to one. Pete said, "You've got to see him."

I asked, "How much does it cost? I don't have much money."

"$1,600 for the first visit."

"I can't afford that."

Pete said, "I'll pay it."

Pete called, and he couldn't get me in. Dr. Wayne said that he was completely booked for the next three years.

Pete said to Dr. Wayne, "Do me a favor. If you get a cancellation, will you call me back?"

Dr. Wayne agreed that he would call if anyone canceled, but it was highly unlikely. They hadn't had a cancellation in years.

Thirty minutes later, the phone rang. Someone had canceled their appointment for the next day.

Pete rushed me to San Diego, and I spent five hours at Dr. Wayne's clinic. When he was finished, he sat me down together with Pete in his office and said, "Charlie, you have an aneurysm, your heart is enlarged, and the left side of your heart is severely blocked. You could die before you leave my office."

"What can I do?" I asked.

He said, "Take these pills." He handed me a bunch of pills.

"Where do you live?" he asked.

"Pensacola, Florida."

"How are you getting there?"

"I'm flying."

"Oh, no you're not," he said. "I want you back here in two weeks." He got up from behind his desk and walked behind me. "I'm not going to charge you," Dr. Wayne said to Pete.

Pete told me later that he was astonished by Dr. Wayne's generosity. I went back two or three times every year, and he never charged Pete or me a penny.

I got better, and then Dr. Wayne retired. After that, I got worse. I'd get out of bed in the morning, walk to the kitchen, and pass out. Jeanne took me to the hospital in Pensacola, and the doctor ran a series of tests on me.

When the test results came back, the doctor said, "Charlie, God has healed your heart. You don't have an aneurysm, your heart is normal in size, and there is no blockage."

The only thing wrong with me was that I was anemic. After a few units of blood and some iron pills, I felt like I was twenty years old again. I went back to work at St. Anne's Church, serving food for twelve hours a day. My only complaint was that my feet hurt at the end of the day.

When I tell people about how God healed me, he gets the glory. He can work out all things for good. I didn't have to worry over what was wrong with my heart. God knew what he wanted to do with that illness. Even if I had died from those heart problems, it wouldn't have mattered. It was a win-win situation. In this life, I'm a child of God, and he loves me unconditionally. He has sent Jesus to cover over all my sins. My joy, peace, and righteousness are complete in him. If I had died, I would have gone to be with Jesus in his glory for all eternity.

■ α ■

**When I tell people about how God healed me, he gets the glory.**

■ Ω ■

## Jeanne Talks About How She Has Grown

After we had been in Belize for many years, my mother called me. At the time, she was 91 years old. I heard her on the phone saying, "This is your mama."

I could not believe it was my mama and that she would pick up the phone and dial all those numbers all by herself. She was very lonely.

She said, "Jeanne, I really want you to come back home."

My mother was by herself, and she could hardly write anymore. Her health was good, and she was able to maintain her house, but she could not drive. She was used to having me go over to her place every morning and have my coffee with her. I wrote all her bills and letters for her, too. There was no one to take that over for me after we went to Belize. She and I had often gone out to dinner, and she missed our time together.

She said on the phone, "When are you coming home?"

I said, "Not for a while." I knew I had to stay with Charlie in Belize.

Being in Belize and away from my family made me look at my own heart. God wanted me to break away from everything and think about myself for once, but it was hard. I began to think, *why am I the way I am?* I concluded that we had always been a very close family, and I suppose it was because of the way I was raised. I am so close to all my kids and grandchildren, just as my mother is close to her kids and grandchildren.

> ■ α ■
> **We must love the members of our families first.**
> ■ Ω ■

For many years, Charlie and I traveled all over the United States, loving people into the kingdom of God. The most important thing I learned from all of our experiences is that we must love the members of our families first with God's love. I John 4:19–21 reads,

> We love because he first loved us. If anyone says, "I love God," yet hates his brother, he is a liar. For anyone who does not love his brother, whom he has seen, cannot love God, whom he has not seen. And he has given us this command: Whoever loves God must also love his brother.

Anyway, Mama said, "Why don't you come home and let Charlie commute back and forth? He can come home once in a while."

That was not the answer. I needed to stay put in Belize. Charlie needed my help.

"Charlie and I will come home like we planned, Mama," I said. "We will see you soon."

One night, as he was preaching, Charlie said, "I don't trust my wife." People looked a little shocked by that statement. He went on to say, "We are not to put our trust in people. We *love* people. We put our *trust* in God."

As I look back on nearly fifty years of marriage with the man to whom I pledged my love, I am filled with gratitude for Charlie. He taught me how to love God. He taught me how to walk in faith and to trust in the Lord.

### Love one another

[11]This is the message you heard from the beginning: We should love one another. [12]Do not be like Cain, who belonged to the evil one and murdered his brother. And why did he murder him? Because his own actions were evil and his brother's were righteous. [13]Do not be surprised, my brothers, if the world hates you. [14]We know that we have passed from death to life, because we love our brothers. Anyone who does not love remains in death. [15]Anyone who hates his brother is a murderer, and you know that no murderer has eternal life in him.

[16]This is how we know what love is: Jesus Christ laid down his life for us. And we ought to lay down our lives for our brothers. [17]If anyone has material possessions and sees his brother in need but has no pity on him, how can the love of God be in him? [18]Dear children, let us not love with words or tongue but with actions and in truth. [19]This then is how we know that we belong to the truth, and how we set our hearts at rest in his presence [20]whenever our hearts condemn us. For God is greater than our hearts, and he knows everything.

[21]Dear friends, if our hearts do not condemn us, we have confidence before God [22]and receive from him anything we ask, because we obey his commands and do what pleases him. [23]And this is his command: to believe in the name of his Son, Jesus Christ, and to love one another as he commanded us. [24]Those who obey his commands live in him, and he in them. And this is how we know that he lives in us: We know it by the Spirit he gave us.

**1 John 3:11–24**

# CHAPTER FIFTEEN

# We Are All Evangelists

## Charlie Looks to the Future

One year after we returned from Belize, Father Jack Gray of St. Anne's Church called me. He wanted me to speak at his parish. I agreed, and when it was time for him to introduce me, he said, "About twenty-five years ago, I was a successful businessman, and I had no intention of giving up what I was doing. And then I heard Charlie Osburn speak. At the age of thirty-eight, I gave up everything I had worked so hard to achieve in my life to give it all to Jesus, just like Charlie did."

I don't have to fight battles with the Catholic Church to reach people with the gospel. God is in charge. The Holy Spirit fights my battles for me. Young people who are thinking about becoming priests or lay evangelists must become aware of this. There will be battles. We often get beaten to pieces.

In this diocese, two priests left because they wanted to marry each other. Another one is in prison because he molested my grandson and some other children. Our church has problems, and they will always be with us.

> ■ α ■
> **Our church has problems, and they will always be with us.**
> ■ Ω ■

But for those who can be obedient to authority and who can take whatever is dished out to them, the Lord will prevail. We can only serve as little, bloody lambs being led to the slaughter. We all turn out to become better people in the end for it. I can look back on my ministry and appreciate what I've been through.

*141*

I don't regret any of the decisions that I made or the conflicts that I encountered. I wouldn't take back what Father Enrico did. It proved that I still had the love of God in my heart, no matter what men wanted to do to stop me from preaching the truth. Today, I've got a pastor who kind of likes me. That doesn't happen very often, and I feel blessed. I am complete.

> **We aren't here to take revenge on others. That's the work of the devil.**

The love of God was proven at the cross. When we can go through the stuff that life dishes out without retaliating, we've learned the whole point of Jesus' message about loving each other. We aren't here to take revenge on others. That's the work of the devil. He's there, waiting for us to tear each other apart.

I feel so wonderful in knowing that thousands of people came to our School of Evangelization over the years. They were baptized in the Holy Spirit and learned what they needed to do with their faith.

The Vatican Council's Decree on the Apostolate of Lay People says this about evangelization:

> The true apostle is on the lookout for occasions of announcing Christ by word, either to unbelievers to draw them toward the faith, or to the faithful to instruct them, strengthen them, incite them to a more fervent life; for Christ's love urges us on.

We are surrounded with 'occasions of announcing Christ by word.' The words we speak to those we live with—our spouses, children, roommates—are such occasions. A warm, loving 'hello and God bless you today' is the best way I know to greet someone in the morning. It announces Christ, if it is sincere and loving. If you're not sincere, you should probably keep quiet. We can announce Christ by sharing our testimonies and telling others what the Lord has done for us.

I was trying to sleep in one Saturday morning, since I had gotten home very late the night before. At about nine o'clock, my wife began singing very loudly in the kitchen in tongues. I grew irritated, because she knew I wanted to sleep. So I tramped down the hall and confronted her.

"What on earth is going on?" I asked.

"The washing machine is broken," she said.

"Why does that make you happy?"

"Because I get to tell the repairman about the love of Jesus."

Every time we encounter someone, whether it's in our home or theirs, in a store or on a bus, we have an opportunity to 'announce Christ by word.' It can be a very short word, such as "Hello, God bless you." Or, if the opportunity presents itself, it can be a full-blown witness about Jesus. The important thing is that we be open to the Holy Spirit and allow him to direct us.

People in need are often the most open to hearing about Christ. Be on the lookout for people who are distressed, hungry, or sick. When we experience Jesus and have a personal relationship with him, it's easy to tell others about him. We can say, "He's my brother, my Savior, my deliverer, my comfort, my joy, my enthusiasm, my excitement, my everything."

I was on my way to San Jose a number of years ago, and I was talking to an engineer who had a heart condition. On the way there, I got to thinking, *there is only one reason that this man could be sitting in this airplane with me. And that's to give his life to Jesus.*

I asked him, "Have you ever opened your heart and confessed Jesus Christ as your Lord and Savior?"

He said, "I haven't."

I asked him, "Would you like to?"

"When?"

"Right now."

We were up at about 12,000 feet. He looked out the window of that airplane and said, "Yeah, it seems like a good time."

Evangelization is not a technique, a plan, or a program. It is a willingness to live the life of Christ and a decision to do so. When you are open, loving, patient, and kind in whatever you do, living the love of Jesus and speaking about it; you are an evangelist.

One day, our granddaughter, Megan, who was two-and-a-half years old, was taken to the doctor for a check-up. One of the first things the doctor said to her was, "Megan, I'm going to check your heart."

"That's where Jesus lives," she told him. "Jesus lives in my heart, and he loves me."

> **Be on the lookout for people who are distressed, hungry, or sick.**

> **Evangelization is not a technique, a plan, or a program.**

That's incredible! At two years of age, Megan was already witnessing for Jesus. Why? Her family had taught her that she is a child of King Jesus. She knew who she was. The same cannot be said for most Christians. Unfortunately, many of them do not understand who they are.

A few weeks after this incident, Jeanne took Megan on a shopping trip to a large department store. A woman shopping nearby was pushing a stroller with a screaming baby in it. This poor, harried mother could not get the child to stop screaming.

Megan quietly slipped out of her grandmother's grasp. Suddenly, the crying stopped. Jeanne looked around, and there was Megan, with her hands on the baby's head. She was praying in tongues. Whatever had been annoying that child vanished with Megan's prayer, and everyone was able to continue shopping peacefully.

Megan was really not an extraordinary two-year-old. She simply said and did the things that all Christians should say and do—children and adults alike.

When we know who we are and what our purpose in this life is, everything else suddenly begins to make sense. Most Christians know that they are supposed to believe in God, attend church, and do good deeds once in a while in order to get to heaven when they die.

Unfortunately, most Christians do not act like people who know who they are. Their knowledge of God and Jesus is frequently limited. They attend church because they know they should. They try to be honest, truthful, and fair, because these are the right things to do. They contribute money to the church and to the poor, because they know this pleases God.

> ■ α ■
> **Christian life is far more than a ritualized set of actions based on a system of intellectual beliefs.**
> ■ Ω ■

While there is nothing wrong with any of these things, they are only a good beginning in our walk with Christ. As responses to the grace and mercy that God has so lovingly poured out on us in Christ Jesus and his church, they are simply inadequate. Christian life is far more than a ritualized set of actions based on a system of intellectual beliefs. A life in Christ is a thrilling daily walk with the most wonderful, the most powerful, the most appealing person in the entire universe. It is tremendously exciting to discover who you are, where you came from, and where you are going. When you walk in this knowledge, you walk with greater boldness, with more zip in your step. You enjoy true peace and the conviction that every day of your life has a real purpose.

Many Christians have given their hearts and lives to the Lord, but they do not experience this kind of assurance. They are burdened with problems. They are afraid to talk to their friends and neighbors about the Lord. They are often angry or impatient with their spouses or children. Material things still tug at their hearts and distract them from serving God.

We constantly receive mail from people who write to say that they have attended a parish meeting where I have spoken or who have listened to my tapes. They often tell me stories about how they became lay evangelists. My vision continues to be fulfilled long after I have spoken with people. I may give up on a person, but the Holy Spirit never stops working in his heart.

I now find it very difficult to talk about the weather or the government. Topics like these bore me. They change. They usually disappoint us. But Jesus is exciting, and Jesus never changes. He never disappoints. Now that I base everything I do on him, on his word, and on his love, life is thrilling, challenging, and rewarding.

A short time after we returned from Belize, Father Gray asked me to establish an international Catholic School of Evangelization at St. Anne's parish in Pensacola, Florida. He offered me office space in his building, free of charge. It is furnished, and it is much nicer than the space that we occupied at St. Anthony's School. Today, our work continues at Good News Ministries, sponsored by St. Anne's Church.

We are excited to be back in Pensacola, and we will be walking in faith to share the love of Jesus Christ to everyone who needs it. Today, in the School of Evangelization, I teach people that the best way—the only way—to evangelize is to love people into the kingdom. When we are patient, kind, gentle, and self-controlled, we manifest the love of Jesus. And when others see the love of Jesus in us, they can more easily believe what we say.

What is our message at our School of Evangelization? We share what God has shown us in our walk with him. We present our testimonies and speak about walking in faith. We tell about patience and

> ■ α ■
> **A life in Christ is a thrilling daily walk with the most wonderful, powerful, appealing person in the entire universe.**
> ■ Ω ■

love, about the lay person's role in the church, and the gifts of the Holy Spirit. Everyone who attends the seminar or listens to the tapes is invited to give his or her life to Jesus Christ and to follow him as an active lay man or woman in the church.

Our goals are very simple. We want to open the doors of spiritual experience to Catholics, and we expect them to walk through those doors and encounter the Lord. By the end of the school, most participants have committed their lives to Jesus, been baptized in the Holy Spirit, and received the gift of tongues. If they then commit themselves to prayer, to reading the Scriptures and the Vatican Council's Decree on the Apostolate of Lay People, the Lord will show them what to do next.

For nearly twenty years, Good News Ministries has given away countless copies of the Vatican Council's Decree on the Apostolate of Lay People and an equal number of sets of audio tapes from our School of Evangelization. Today, many of our messages are available for download from the internet.

Everyone who follows this simple decree sooner or later finds God prompting them to tell others what he has done for them. This is evangelization—spreading the good news of the love and mercy of Jesus. Jesus commands us in Matthew 28:18,

> Therefore go and make disciples of all nations, baptizing them in the name of the Father and of the Son and of the Holy Spirit, and teaching them to obey everything I have commanded you. And surely I am with you always, to the very end of the age.

The teaching of Scripture and the church make it very clear: we *must* evangelize. We must tell others about the Lord.

During our week-long School of Evangelization, we explain our needs and ask the people to make a donation, if they feel so moved. From time to time, we mention special needs, as we did when we were purchasing our television equipment or repairing our bus. That is all the fund-raising we do. We allow the Holy Spirit to move in people's hearts, and we have never been disappointed. God has supplied every need, because we have followed him in faith.

■ α ■

**We *must* evangelize.**

■ Ω ■

The gospels tell us about the life and teachings of Jesus. They reveal to us a faith we should believe in and a teaching to follow. But there is more to the gospels than we realize.

Jesus was excited about who he was, and he was excited about his mission. I can just imagine Jesus shouting with happiness as he preached the Good News, thrilled when someone embraced his message.

The men and women who met Jesus and who believed in his teaching were completely changed by their experiences. The gospels tell us about many of them. Peter was an uneducated fisherman who was headstrong and chicken-hearted. But Jesus changed him. The prostitute who was about to be stoned listened to Jesus. He changed her. The sick, the blind, the poor in faith—Jesus changed them all.

All of these people had to *do* something in order to be changed. They had to meet Jesus, listen to his teaching, and believe in him and his words. When they did, it revolutionized their lives. They suddenly had new meaning and purpose. These people were happy! They were thrilled with what Jesus had done for them, and they eagerly shared that Good News with others.

> **All of these people had to *do* something in order to be changed.**

The gospels tell us that we are to be like that, too. We are to meet Jesus personally and give our lives to him. We are to live as sons and daughters of God. We are part of Jesus' mission to save the human race, to actively work with him to bring truth, joy, and peace to the men and women he brings to us. It could not be more clear.

God has chosen each of us, no matter how unlikely we seem, to be an important part of Jesus' mission in the world. God is not looking for a genius. All he wants is a willing heart. And all we need to do is say, "Yes, Lord, pull me through that knothole. Strip off my pride, Lord. Remove my selfishness. Give me a spirit of love, and let me see people the way you see them."

I spoke earlier about fear. When we accept the Lord and begin to live in a state of faith, we no longer need to be afraid. All we need to do is turn to the Lord, identify our fears, and cast them out in the name of Jesus. Are you afraid of failure? Cast it out. There are no failures in the kingdom of God, only saints redeemed by Jesus Christ. Are you afraid of losing your money? Cast out that fear. You don't need money to be happy—you need Jesus. Once you have Jesus in your life, you'll never be in want of anything. He'll take care of you. Are you timid, afraid of facing life head on? Cast it out. Jesus wants you to be a bold Christian, filled with joy and fervor for sharing the good news of salvation with others.

> **There are no failures in the kingdom of God.**

When you identify your fears as best you can, get down on your knees and pray, "Go away, Satan, and take your spirit of fear with you. I am a child of God, redeemed by the blood of Jesus. You no longer have any hold over me."

Then let Jesus fill you with faith, hope, and love. You will be free from fear. You may sometimes be tempted to let fear creep back into your life, but when this happens, rebuke it. Tell Satan that, like John in the book of Revelation, you have seen the Lord, and he told you "there is nothing to fear." Satan can't tolerate that kind of talk. He'll be gone as quickly as if you had jabbed him with a hot poker.

When we are free of fear, we can do what God wants us to do. We can live in his love, and we can spread that love around by evangelizing. That's why we are on this earth in the first place, and when we get busy with the job, not only does fear stay far away, but so do a lot of other problems. If we are busy evangelizing, we won't have time for greed, envy, laziness, or lust. We'll be too busy loving to have time for sinning. Does this sound simplistic? Too good to be true? Give it a try!

When Catholic lay people—men, women, boys, and girls—take on this attitude, we will see this wonderful church evangelize the entire world. What could be more exciting than that?

# A Personal Message to the Reader

Perhaps you have not allowed Jesus to be the Lord of your life. Or you may have made a decision for him at one time, but have not stuck with it. Perhaps you haven't experienced the great thrill of allowing the Holy Spirit to possess you, to own you, and to control you. If you haven't yet done it, I urge you to make a commitment to Jesus right now—right where you are. If you want to live for Jesus, turn to him by praying this simple prayer:

> Lord Jesus, by faith I turn to you now. I ask you to give me the joy and peace of knowing you. I want you to come into my life and be my Lord and Savior. I ask you to deliver me from the things of this world that stand between you and me. I need you, Lord Jesus. Fill me with your Holy Spirit so that I may live my life as a child of God. I want to be free of sin, free of the attacks of Satan, and free of sickness. Come, Lord Jesus, be my Lord and Savior. Amen.

**Perhaps you haven't experienced the Holy Spirit.**

To enjoy true peace and the conviction that our lives have a real purpose, we need to start behaving in a new way. When we do, God gives us the grace to make it. The first step is to read and to pray. We find out who we are and what God wants us to do with our lives. A great deal of godly wisdom is contained in the gospels and in the Second Vatican Council's Decree on the Apostolate of Lay People. After

**We must take action.**

some study and prayer, we must take action. A pastor or an active Christian lay person is sure to have some good advice.

If, after reading this book, you would like to learn more about our School of Evangelization or how you can have a closer relationship with Jesus, we would like to help you. Our website is www.romancatholicevangelization.com. You can download all of our tapes and listen to nearly fifty talks about how Jesus wants to change your life. You will also find more information there about our School of Evangelization. We do not charge anything for you to attend our school or to receive our literature. If you have further questions after visiting our website, please email us at claborn1@yahoo.com or call 850-456-0142.

> **You are a unique, marvelous creation of the almighty God.**

And remember, you are a unique, marvelous creation of the almighty God. He created the entire universe and you for his enjoyment, and he wants to have a personal relationship with you through his son, Jesus Christ. It doesn't matter who you are, where you've been, or what you've done. The Holy Spirit can overcome anything in your life.

After you find out how good it feels to have the love of Jesus and the power of the Holy Spirit lighting you up inside, you won't be able to stop telling people about him and how he has changed your life. Every one of you was born to become an evangelist, and it's up to you to tell all of your brothers and sisters just how good God is.

> **Every one of you was born to become an evangelist.**

If you think your life will never change, remember that an angel once told a teenage girl named Mary, "Nothing is impossible with God." (Luke 1:37) I never would have believed that change was possible for me, but look what God has done!

Praise the Lord!

—*Charlie Osburn*

# Epilogue

*By Cheryl Denton, Editor*

I knew very little about Charlie Osburn before I set out to work on this book, except for a short tale that my friend, Harvey Whitney, had told me several years ago. I had noticed a picture in Harvey's office of some guy standing next to Mother Teresa. When I asked about that guy, Harvey told me that there were some amazing events in the man's life that had caused him to give up everything he had worked to achieve in order to tell the world about Jesus. The man's name was Charlie Osburn.

As I began the work on this book, I listened to Charlie's tapes, read his materials, and talked to him by phone. In the process, the Holy Spirit began to work in me. I now know a great deal about Charlie and how he came alongside Mother Teresa to serve people who were physically and spiritually dying. I found out why he is so excited about telling everyone in the world that Jesus loves them. I have a story of my own that has resulted from working with Charlie.

I have known about Jesus since I was about four years old, when my parents began taking me to worship services and Sunday school every week without fail. I raised my four children in the church, and my husband is a hospital chaplain. I was baptized as an infant and then again through immersion on my fortieth birthday. You would think that I would be an all-together Christian. Whenever we went to church, though, everyone else seemed really happy. I would just sit and cry through most services. Something was missing inside of me.

For the past four years, I have struggled with multiple sclerosis. Over time, the flare-ups grew worse until I had to rely on an electric wheelchair to get around whenever I left the house. On the day

Harvey Whitney called me about working on this book, I had gotten out of bed for the first time in six days. Unbearable pain in my left leg had made it impossible for me to put any weight on it. I had been using a walker to get from my bed to my bathroom, and my daughters were bringing meals to me in my bed. For several years, I was only able to sit up at my desk for a couple of hours a day before I became too exhausted to work.

Harvey had given me a deadline for finishing this book, due to an upcoming conference where Charlie would be speaking. I knew that if I wanted to make that deadline, I would have to work more than two hours a day. I knew that something in my life had to change.

I was still getting around the house in a wheelchair when I began to read Charlie's first book, *The Charlie Osburn Story*. That was on a Friday. By Sunday, I wondered if the Holy Spirit could change me as it had changed Charlie. I wanted what Charlie was talking about.

On Monday morning, I lay in my bed and began praying, "Jesus, I have tried every doctor, pill, and treatment there is for my pain. I cannot deal with this illness any longer. I am giving it to you." I paused, then said, "Holy Spirit, fill me with your power and light. Please give me the strength that I had in my youth." I continued praying, but I felt that there was something blocking my prayers. I remembered something Charlie had said about rebuking Satan. So I said, "Satan, in the name of Jesus Christ, I rebuke all the pain and weakness that you have brought into my body. Leave me alone!" I felt the need to breathe deeply, and as soon as I exhaled, my arms and legs jerked as if I were having a mild seizure.

Immediately, I thought, *wow, that was weird*. In the next instant, I thought, *no, it was the power of the Holy Spirit*.

I sat up and swung my legs over the side of the bed and wiggled my toes. For the first time in months, my toes actually moved. I rotated my feet at the ankles. They worked! I stood up carefully and slowly eased my weight onto my left leg. No pain! I looked at myself in the full length mirror at the other end of the room. I was standing up without a walker! A big grin spread over my face, and I did a little dance along the side of the bed. I raised my arms over my head and high-stepped around the end of the bed. Every muscle and joint in my body moved like it had when I was a teenager.

"Thank you, Jesus!" I said. All I wanted to do at that point was spend every moment praising Jesus for bringing me into his kingdom. Worship music exalting the name of Jesus began running through my mind.

On Tuesday, I repeated my prayer to the Holy Spirit, asking for healing in every cell of my body. I asked him to fill each cell with so much goodness that it would crowd out any illness around it. Again, in the name of Jesus, I rebuked any spirits of illness to leave my body. As before, I felt that same need to breathe deeply, and when I exhaled, my arms and legs jerked, but not quite as long as they had on Monday.

I repeated this process each morning until Friday. When I finished my prayers that day, my fingers and toes only gave a mild twitch. I knew at that point that whatever spirits of illness that had been keeping me from being healed were gone. I lay on my bed, feeling completely relaxed and at peace. A wonderful sense of light washed over my entire body and seemed to fill the room. I never wanted to move, and once again, I began to hear praise music in my mind. On that day, my faith was renewed by the power of the Holy Spirit.

The following day, our family left to travel to the mountains in North Carolina, where our son would be attending college. We decided to go on a hike to a waterfall. I had not been able to walk from our house to the end of our block for the past several years. On that day, I trekked two miles over uneven terrain, uphill and down. The only pain I felt was the next-day stiffness of muscles that had not been used in years.

Every morning since then, I have awakened to various praise songs in my head, even though I have not heard some of them in ages. I feel so energized and renewed by the power of the Holy Spirit and the love of Jesus that I have been able to write for ten or twelve hours a day. The time has flown by, and I have not wanted to stop working with Charlie on this book. I'm excited about telling others how wonderful it feels to be all lit up inside by God's love.

Some people question whether or not Jesus has given all believers authority to rebuke demons and command them to leave. Luke 9:1 reads, "When Jesus had called the Twelve together, he gave them power and authority to drive out all demons and to cure diseases, and he sent them out to preach the kingdom of God and to heal the sick." Jesus later sent seventy-two messengers ahead of him into every town where he was going to visit. Luke 10:17 tells us, "The seventy-two returned with joy and said, 'Lord, even the demons submit to us in your name.'"

Some believers may have difficulty accepting that they have this power, because Jesus replied to those seventy-two in Luke 10:18, "I saw Satan fall like lightning from heaven. I have given you authority to trample on snakes and scorpions and to overcome all the power of the enemy; nothing will harm you. However, do not rejoice that the spirits submit to you, but rejoice that your names are written in heaven." In other words, Jesus was saying it's okay to rebuke the spirits, as long as we don't become proud and begin to boast that we are the ones who are empowered to make them leave. We should be most thankful for our salvation through Christ.

In a few days, we will be leaving for our first family vacation in five years. We have not gone anywhere, partly because I have been too ill to travel, and partly because we have spent most of our money on medical expenses. We are planning to start out at an amusement park, and I intend to ride a roller coaster. I am *not* taking my wheelchair.

I hope that you will be blessed by the stories that Charlie has to tell. And when you finish reading, I pray that you will share this book with someone else. It's a story that can change the world, one soul at a time.